D1634869

THE REMNANT

BOURNEMOUTH LIBRARIES

630043438 V

This book is dedicated to my descendants — in memory of the 8,000 Jews of Dubno, including my parents, whom the Germans shot and buried in mass graves.

THE REMNANT

On Burning Wings – To a Displaced Persons Camp and Beyond

Michael G. Kesler, Ph.D

With Foreword by Glenn Dynner,
Professor of Religion at Sarah Lawrence College,
Guggenheim Fellow

VALLENTINE MITCHELL
LONDON • CHICAGO

First published in 2021 by Vallentine Mitchell

Catalyst House,
720 Centennial Court,
Centennial Park, Elstree WD6 3SY, UK

814 N. Franklin Street,
Chicago, Illinois
60610 USA

www.vmbooks.com

Copyright © 2021 Michael G. Kesler

British Library Cataloguing in Publication Data:
An entry can be found on request

ISBN 978 1 912676 63 7 (Paper)
ISBN 978 1 912676 64 4 (Ebook)

Library of Congress Cataloging in Publication Data:
An entry can be found on request

All rights reserved. No part of this publication may be reproduced in any form or by any means, electronic, mechanical, photocopying, reading or otherwise, without the prior permission of Vallentine Mitchell & Co. Ltd.

Contents

Acknowledgements

An apocryphal story tells of Lot and his wife fleeing Sodom and Gomorrah. Lot warns his wife not to look back lest they both be consumed by the conflagration. The wife does look back and turns into a pillar of salt.

'Don't go to the mass graves,' my sister Luba warned me. 'Stop reading about the catastrophe. We need to move on, we need to move on,' she urged. And I, like most survivors, kept mum for many years about the greatest calamity to befall the Jews.

The wake-up calls came from the Nuremberg Trials of the Nazi hierarchy and the 1961 trial of the captured Eichmann. Their outrageous lies, denials and presumed righteousness shook me to the core. Primo Levi's *Survival in Auschwitz* (1947), Elie Wiesel's *Night* (1960), and other chronicles of the Holocaust – these accounts were etched deeply into my mind and soul.

And, although preoccupied with my profession and raising a family and building a home, they compelled me to revisit the past and write about the six most painful years in my life: my experiences during the Second World War. I retired in 2006 due to glaucoma-induced loss of vision. This opened the door, in time and focus, for me to look back on that haunting period.

It gave rise to my book *Shards of War* in 2010. The book had a pretty good run. It got a great number of 5-star reviews on Amazon. It received high praise from academics, prominent among them Professors Atina Grossmann of Cooper Union, and Curt Leviant and Paul Hanebrink of Rutgers University.

The 2010 publication of *Shards of War* led me to extend my writing to my experiences in the Landsberg Displaced Persons camp. This released a floodgate of memories of other earth- and peace-shaking events that happened after I left the camp, such as: the break-up of the Second World War alliance between the West and the Soviet Union; the beginning of the Cold War, the accounting of the six million Jewish victims and the tragic state of the Jewish survivors, among others.

Five years of research on these subjects gave birth to *The Remnant*. Lucy S. Dawidowicz's book *The War Against the Jews: 1933–1945* (1975) and Sir

Martin Gilbert's book *The Holocaust: A History of the Jews of Europe During the Second World War* (1985), among others, served as the springboards for my research.

I acknowledge author and playwright Brent Monahan for his tireless efforts to prepare the manuscript's first draft. I owe William Greenleaf, whom we discovered searching for literary services, a big thank you for his masterful line edit. I recognize the tremendous help of Suzanne Scara, my unusually perceptive researcher and extraordinarily creative secretary, who nurtured the manuscript from its very birth to completion.

I am grateful to Omer Bartov, John P. Birkelund Distinguished Professor of European History, Brown University, and Manus Midlarsky, Moses and Annuta Back Professor of International Peace and Conflict Resolution, Rutgers University, for their roles as peer readers and critics. They offered their expert advice and helped me mould the book into a more scholarly form. I express my deep gratitude to the noted historian and Guggenheim Fellow, Professor Glenn Dynner of Sarah Lawrence College, for the Foreword. It distills the introductory material and rich backdrop, clarifies the remnant's meaning and propels the book to a more solid academic level.

I'm much obliged to Vallentine Mitchell, the publisher of this book. I tip my hat to Toby Harris whose creativity and management skills secured the printing of my manuscript on time despite the difficulties caused by the pandemic. I'd also like to thank Lisa Hyde for her guidance and prompt assistance throughout the editing process.

My wife, Dr. Barbara S. Reed, served as my resident consultant-in-need through all hours of day and night, to whom I owe extra hugs and kisses.

About the Author

Michael G. Kesler, a Ph.D chemical engineer graduate of MIT and NYU, had a more than half-century career in the petroleum industry. During his tenure with M.W. Kellogg, he published in 1958 a seminal paper on the use of computers in oil refining design. Later, at Mobil Oil, he co-authored a series of publications on thermodynamics that starred on the list of most-referenced papers in the hundred-year history of the *AIChE Journal*. A decade later, as founder and president of his own consulting firm, he pioneered the use of personal computers for equipment design in the petroleum refining industry. His research and consulting activities opened the door for his process engineering work in the revamp and design of a number of refinery units in the United States, Canada and Europe.

In 2006, he retired due to vision loss as a result of glaucoma. Since that time, he has written several books on his and his late wife's Second World War experiences. *The Remnant* addresses episodes of his life during the Second World War and its immediate aftermath.

The author and his wife, Barbara S. Reed, Ph.D, professor emerita of journalism at Rutgers University, live in East Brunswick, New Jersey. They proudly head a family of six children and eleven grandchildren. Barbara and Michael lead an active social and cultural life and belong to several community organizations. The East Brunswick Public Library, at its recent annual gala, honoured Michael with a legacy award for his contributions to the community.

Foreword

By Glenn Dynner, Professor of Religion at
Sarah Lawrence College and Guggenheim Fellow

In the fall of 1939, German and Soviet troops invaded Poland from both sides and divided the country between them. Roughly 1.5 million Polish Jews found themselves in the comparatively better Soviet zone. Around one-fifth were subsequently expelled by the Soviets as 'unreliable elements' or, like 16-year old Michael Kesler, decided to flee before the Nazi invasion of the Soviet zone on 22 June 1941. Most of the remaining Jewish population was murdered by German mobile killing squads and their local volunteers – shot over pits in forests on the outskirts of their towns and buried in mass graves in what has been called 'the Holocaust by bullets'.[1] A small contingent survived the war in hiding with their neighbours, fighting as forest partisans or serving as soldiers in the Red Army. On 6 July 1945, Polish Jews who had survived the war in Soviet territories were given the choice of Soviet or Polish citizenship. Those who chose the former would have to endure life under an increasingly anti-Jewish Stalin, who lethally targeted Jewish cultural figures, 'cosmopolites', and doctors.[2] The roughly 231,000 Jews who chose Polish citizenship fared little better, meeting with hostility as they attempted to reclaim their homes, and full-fledged pogroms in the cases of Kielce, Kraków and Rzeszów.[3] Many Polish Jews thus continued on, gathering first in Displaced Persons camps and settling finally in Israel, America and other new centres.

Throughout the ordeal, Michael Kesler seems to have made all the right choices. Yet as his compelling memoir shows, even the best choices were often accompanied by a deep sense of shame and guilt. A native of the storied town of Dubno, Michael found himself in the Soviet occupation zone and drafted into the Red Army. Convinced he would be used as cannon fodder, he deserted. This was his first tormenting decision. After living out the war years in Samarkand, Uzbekistan, Michael then made the difficult decision to abandon Samarkand and his first love, a local woman named Mahdu, and return to Poland.

Arriving in Lviv (formerly Lwów), Michael and his sister learned of the mass executions of their parents and the rest of the Dubno Jewish community, which had occurred in two main phases in 1942. When they finally arrived at their family's house, its new Ukrainian inhabitant cursed them and chased them away. A visit to a mass grave did the rest and Michael resolved to leave for good. 'Though overcome by the guilt of having lived through the slaughter,' he writes, 'I accepted it as a necessary burden I would have to carry, even as I moved forward'.

Michael's journey forward took him through a Displaced Persons camp, a stint in Paris and finally to America, Colby College and MIT. Thanks to his extraordinary intellectual gifts and uncanny perseverance, he was able not only to forge a successful career as a chemical engineer and create a wonderful family life, but also raise public awareness about the lost East-European Jewish past. Michael wrote books, sponsored lectures and concerts and performed timeless Yiddish songs in order to convey the unique Jewish civilization that had preceded the Holocaust.

His current memoir adds a new dimension to our understanding: the quandaries involved in the very choices that enabled him to survive the destruction of European Jewry.

Notes

1. Patrick Desbois, *The Holocaust by Bullets: A Priest's Journey to Uncover the Truth Behind the Murder of 1.5 Million Jews* (St. Martin's Griffin, 2009); Wendy Lower, *Nazi Empire-Building and the Holocaust in Ukraine* (University of North Carolina Press, 2006).
2. On the 'Night of the Murdered Poets', which involved the execution of thirteen Soviet Jewish writers on 12 August 1952, see Jefferey Rubenstein and Vladimir Naumov (Eds), *Stalin's Secret Pogrom: The Postwar Inquisition of the Jewish Anti-Fascist Committee* (New Haven: Yale University Press, 2001). On the Doctor's Plot, see Jonathan Brent and Vladimir P. Naumov, *Stalin's Last Crime: The Plot Against the Jewish Doctors, 1948–1953* (NY: HarperCollins, 2001).
3. Gennady Estraikh, 'Flight through Poland: Soviet Jewish Emigration in the 1950s', *Jewish History* 31 (2018), 291–317. Jewish casualties are hard to estimate, but were in the hundreds. See Jan Gross, *Fear: Anti-Semitism in Poland after Auschwitz: An Essay in Historical Interpretation* (NJ: Princeton University Press, 2006); Anna Cichopek-Gajraj and Glenn Dynner, 'Pogroms in Modern Poland, 1918-1946', in Elissa Bemporad and Eugene Avrutin (Eds), *Pogroms: A Documentary History* (NY: Oxford University Press, forthcoming).

Preface

The sun peered through the window of my East Brunswick, New Jersey abode, caressing my face, on 6 July 2015. I smacked my lips with delight as the aroma of pancakes teased my nostrils: My wife, Barbara, was preparing pancakes for my ninetieth birthday. Suddenly, pain pierced my heart and tightened my chest. I slid down my bed, but could not stand up. My legs became rubbery. I shivered with panic as I passed out. Fifteen minutes later, strong arms carried me out to the waiting ambulance. Half an hour later, I lay panting for breath in the Critical Care Unit of the local hospital.

I had suffered a heart attack due to internal bleeding. I also had blood clots, one of which had migrated to my lung. The medicine the doctors administered failed to stop the bleeding, indicating the need for surgical intervention. The cardiologist asked for my medical directive for resuscitation, if needed; I refused to supply it, which put to rest the talk of surgery.

On the fourth day of my illness, my lungs filled with fluid. I could barely breathe or speak, with or without an oxygen mask. The family gathered, and we spent a few hours discussing the ordering of my affairs and my preferred funeral arrangements. I had never felt closer to my wife and children.

I slept well that night, and when I awoke, I felt as if I had been transported back to the woods near Lublin in Poland, where my father had worked as a forester. I saw again through the eyes of a four year-old, walking through the woods with Dad and my sister Luba, picking sun-ripened strawberries from the ground and ripe hazelnuts off nearby trees. I was alive and young again. An overwhelming sweetness suffused my body. In the morning my wife Barbara visited me, and as I recounted my elation, I began to laugh with a heartiness I had never experienced. It seemed to come from my whole being rather than just from my throat: I felt my body resonating in unison with a joy I could barely contain. Barbara laughed with me for the longest time until, exhausted, we collapsed into each other's arms. I improved dramatically after that.

My sobering brush with death and the harsh reminder of my mortality compelled me to complete my memoir of Second World War experiences.

Polish Jewry bore the epic brunt of Hitler's war to annihilate the Jews. One tenth of Poland's pre-war 3,000,000 Jews, including my sister and myself, fled Hitler's grasp and lived through the war in the Soviet Union. They became the largest remnant of Polish Jews who survived the Second World War. My sister Luba, myself and a refugee friend personify their plight.

1

The Deserter

On a thief, the hat's on fire.

– Polish proverb

I have searched my memory for where to start winding down the story of my war years. But memory, like dreams, has its own way of marking time and space.

As I pondered, I bumped into one of those markers – personal events etched deeply into my mind that took place more than seven decades ago in a remote corner of the Soviet Union. It was 12 April 1944. My sister, Luba, and I were on a train from Kattakurgan, Uzbekistan, bound for the city of Samarkand. A few hours earlier, I had deserted the Soviet army, fleeing from the base at Kattakurgan where I had trained for several months. Luba, my older sister and only sibling, had fled with me. In fact, she was the one who had so carefully planned my escape.

Now, pretending to be an engineer's assistant in an effort to avoid capture by the military, I was shovelling coal into the locomotive's furnace and trying not to worry about our dire situation.

Three years earlier, Luba and I, still teens, had left our hometown of Dubno in eastern Poland, just ahead of the advancing German armies. We had also left our parents, relatives and friends. Our three-thousand-mile journey by foot and often by jumping onto moving trains, in the midst of the horrific war and bloodshed, had brought us to Uzbekistan. There we had lived and worked as refugees for two years, until I was drafted into the Soviet army.

Now we were on the run again.

The train screeched to a halt in the early morning hours. I stopped shoveling and peered through the coal-blackened window. *Samarkand* was emblazoned in Cyrillic above the main door of the station.

A few moments later, Luba grabbed hold of me. 'Let's go,' she said. 'I gave the engineer some money. It's okay.'

We left the locomotive and walked toward the station. It was still dark. I felt drunk with the fresh air after spending the night in the suffocating engine room. We moved briskly through the crowd of passengers toward the station's bathroom.

'Wait here,' Luba said. She came back a few moments later with a wet newspaper. 'Wipe your face. It's covered with coal dust.'

After I had done so, we ran outside and soon found a horse-drawn wagon for hire.

'Take us to the Old City, and I'll tell you the rest when we get there,' Luba said to the driver as she handed him some roubles.

Suddenly, I began to shiver. The morning chill coursed through my bones, but it was fear and remorse, not cold, that was causing my teeth to chatter. In my mind's eye, I could see the colonel, head of the Kattakurgan base, two days earlier as he addressed our unit of two thousand men headed for the front. He'd drawn our attention to a soldier, allegedly a deserter, hanging by his neck from gallows that had been erected near the barracks.

'That is what will happen to any of you if you try to desert,' he promised.

'*I deserted the army!*' screamed a voice inside my head. '*I committed a crime punishable by death!*'

We stopped at a row of dilapidated houses and stepped off the wagon. A dozen or so rickety stairs took us to a door on the second floor, where Luba fetched a key from her little pocketbook. Her hands shook as she fumbled with the key.

That was when I realized that she was as scared as I was. But even the obvious tension in Luba's words and manner did not hide her beauty. In the few years since we'd left home, her face had become more rounded, her lips fuller and broader, her greyish-green eyes larger and more animated, and her brown braid longer, reaching down to her waist. She was petite and slender, and looked a lot like our mother.

Finally the door creaked open, and we entered a small room scantily furnished with two sofas, a small table, a couple of chairs and a sink. A narrow door opened to a tiny bathroom.

Exhausted, I collapsed onto one of the sofas still fully dressed, and tried to sleep. But I couldn't stop trembling. I expected to hear pounding on the door at any moment, and I kept seeing that limp, pathetic figure dangling from the gallows.

After four gruelling months of training in the Soviet army, Luba had convinced me to desert. I hadn't wanted to listen, but her logic was compelling.

Now, while my exhausted body craved sleep, my brain insisted on going back through the argument we'd had the day before…

***

'Sit down, relax, my brother,' Luba had said during my visit to her room in the village of Kattakurgan. It was a poor excuse for living quarters: dirt floor, white clay walls and little furniture. But we had fared worse over the past three years.

Concerned, I lowered myself into a hardback chair across from her. 'What is it, Luba? Are you ill?'

She shook her head. Her eyes were steady on mine. 'I want to talk to you, and I want you to listen carefully. I have arranged for you to escape from the army compound.'

Her matter-of-fact pronouncement stunned me. 'Escape?' I blinked, sure that I must have misunderstood her. 'From the army?'

'Yes.'

I couldn't believe it. 'Do you know what you're saying?' I yelled.

She didn't flinch from my reaction or my widened eyes. 'Mekhel, I know what I'm telling you to do is very dangerous, but going to the front is no less dangerous. I have arranged everything for your safe escape. I was able to get you a new passport, and I have a room for us in Samarkand.'

'Samarkand?' The city was about a hundred miles north of Kattakurgan. 'How in the world would we get there?'

'By train. I have it all figured out. All I want you to do is to have a little faith and a little courage.'

I shook my head vigorously. 'I have never committed a crime, and what you're asking me to do is criminal, punishable by death. Even if the army fails to catch me and hang me, I will feel ashamed and guilty all my life.'

'You are not being realistic. You think that you'll go to the front and kill a few Germans, avenging their mass murder of millions of innocent Jews, possibly including our parents. But that isn't you, Mekhel. You have never learned to fight, to hate, to murder somebody. If the Soviets had any decency, they would have never picked *you* to be a foot soldier. You're short and scrawny. You'll be no match for a German soldier in combat. The army will use *you* to sweep for mines, and they won't care when you're blown up. They'll replace you with somebody else whose life is expendable.'

'Where did you get that crazy idea?'

'It's not a crazy idea. You'll soon see it for yourself – young men in wheelchairs with missing arms and legs. They're all coming here from the front.' She blinked away sudden tears. 'I don't want my brother to be blown up. I want you to live. You're probably the only remaining male member of Father's and Mother's families. You have a right to live. You have an *obligation* to live.'

I wanted to deny what Luba said, but I was beginning to see her point. Before leaving for the army, I had been surer of myself. But the last few months of training had taught me a lot about my own physical limitations.

Luba saw that I was hesitating. 'Mekhel, we have no time to waste. There's a train leaving for Samarkand in an hour. If we don't catch that train, you'll have to return to the barracks and go to the front. Please listen to me. I want you to live. I want both of us to return home safely someday. Like all wars before it, this one will eventually end. We'll survive, and maybe we'll find Mother and Father alive. Can you imagine how happy they will be to see us again?'

I swallowed and looked away so she wouldn't see my own tears.

'Take off your army uniform and put on the clothes I prepared for you,' she commanded.

I got up slowly and did as she asked, and in a few minutes I was ready to go. Luba had her belongings packed in a bundle. She gave me my new passport, then hid my army uniform under the bed and tidied up the room. A moment later we were running through the narrow, empty streets to the train station, where we boarded the train to Samarkand.

***

I woke up from a fitful sleep and saw through the window of the apartment that the large red sun was lifting slowly above the few shacks next to ours.

Luba soon awoke as well. 'I'll run down and get something to eat,' she said. She soon came back with two small *lepyoshka* flatbreads. She heated up a pot of water, and we sat down at the tiny table. 'Drink some hot tea,' she said. 'You're shivering.'

'I'm not cold,' I said. 'I'm angry.'

She frowned at me. 'What are you so angry about?'

'I shouldn't have run away.'

She sighed. 'Do we have to go through this again? You think you would have gone to the front, killed some Germans and become a hero?'

'I feel like a traitor. I betrayed the country that gave us shelter.'

'You speak as if you were a native Russian. We are Polish, and they didn't even have the right to draft you.'

'Shame will haunt me for the rest of my life.'

'So be ashamed, but be alive,' Luba said, starting to cry.

I fell silent. After all, there was no going back. Now I had to focus on not being caught. I did not want to end up swinging from the gallows at the army base with the colonel watching. And I knew that if we were caught, Luba would be swinging next to me. Then I had an epiphany: *I must leave the city and go to a farm. That will keep me out of the army's grasp.*

Before I had been drafted into the army, Luba and I had spent our first two years in Uzbekistan on a farm fifteen miles from Syr Darya, far away from the flames of war. There, I had become a veterinary assistant. The farmers called me Dr. *Bolasi,* the 'boy doctor', and treated me like family. Luba found work as a teacher in the local elementary school. That period had brought us much-needed rest from our flight in the midst of the horrible war. It had brought me, personally, peace of mind and hope.

When I told Luba of my idea that we should go to a farm, she became excited as well. 'I know someone who can help!'

The next day, Luba burst into the apartment with a young man by her side. He was of medium height, with black hair and lively, dark eyes.

'Meet Moniek Perlman,' Luba said. 'You'll go with him to work on a collective farm. It is out in the boondocks, and nobody will bother you there.'

Moniek extended his hand and greeted me in a friendly way.

I gave him my limp hand and weakly answered 'Hello'.

He explained that he was in charge of fixing machinery at the collective farm and would use me as his assistant. That sounded good, but one thing bothered me.

I turned to my sister. 'You will not be coming?'

She shook her head. 'I must stay here in Samarkand so I can work and make some money.'

'When will I see you again?'

'Soon,' she promised.

We embraced, and I felt Luba's tears wetting my cheek.

'Don't worry, Lubushka,' I said, making an effort to resume my protective-brother role. But my brief burst of bravado didn't last. I, too, felt like crying and almost did.

We bade goodbye, and I left for the farm with Moniek.

Soon we were walking silently along a dirt road bordered on each side with lush, budding vegetation of baby cucumbers, squash and other vines and bushes. I was already missing Luba, who had been at my side for the past three years.

Moniek finally broke the uncomfortable silence. 'How did you and Luba manage to get here on your own? You're both so young.'

I decided that talking would be better than thinking and worrying, so I told him how we had left our home two days after the Germans invaded the Soviet Union. It was 24 June 1941. The Germans seemed unstoppable, and they had crossed the border only thirty or so miles from Dubno.

'Only you and Luba escaped?' Moniek asked. 'What about your parents?'

I related how our mother had refused to become a vagabond and how our father had reluctantly remained behind with her. As I spoke, my mind relived the argument that had taken place in our house in Dubno…

***

Luba, flushed and agitated, had sat across the kitchen table from Mother. She had bad news. 'The Germans have broken through the front, and the Russians are fleeing.' She said that her physics professor, a reserve colonel in the Red Army, had told her to urge her family to leave Dubno immediately.

Mother wasn't having it. 'Enough already! Stop your foolish talk. You want me and Father to abandon everything and run away, like crazies?' She reminded Luba of the time, in September 1939, when we had fled, fearing the German advance, and found Ukrainians occupying our home when we returned a week later.

Memories flashed in my mind of Messerschmitts overhead strafing us as we lay flat on the dusty road. The German Army, having subdued the Polish Cavalry in blitzkrieg fashion, moved in to occupy our town in the eastern part of Poland. A few days later, however, the Soviet Army came to replace the Germans, as per the famous Molotov-Ribbentrop Pact of 23 August 1939. So we soon returned home and became citizens of the Soviet Union for the next two years.

'This is different,' Luba said sharply. 'The Germans are coming. We have a choice. We can leave, or we can stay here and wait to be killed.'

Mother shook her head in denial. 'We met the Austrians and some Germans during World War I, and we lived on. It was the Ukrainian Petlura and his gangs who killed my brother at the end of the war!' With that her stiff demeanour collapsed, and she broke down and cried. Mother had often told us of her daring mission to ransom the severed head of her brother,

Mekhel, from Petlura's gang. My uncle, whose name I bore, a lawyer and socialist leader in town, had been Mother's favourite sibling.

In the midst of the argument and tears there at our kitchen table, Father returned from morning prayers at the shul. His face was ashen and sweaty, his eyes bloodshot and bulging. It was a sharp contrast to the quiet, even-tempered man I had always known, and it frightened me.

'What's the matter, Moyne?' Mother asked with alarm.

'There is a lot of fear and panic,' Father said with uncharacteristic speed, as if rushing to beat time. 'The Germans have broken through the Russian front with lots of tanks. Some people in the shul are preparing to leave town.' He drew a breath as though trying to calm himself. 'We must gather whatever belongings we can and leave before the Germans get here.'

Mother stared at him in disbelief. 'What are we going to do? What are we going to live on? Leave everything and become penniless beggars in a foreign land? And what about the Ukrainians? They have plenty of Jewish blood on their hands. I don't know who are worse, they or Hitler's gangs.'

'Mother, Mother!' Luba screamed. 'How can you say that? You have seen the newspaper stories about the Germans hanging and shooting Jews and building concentration camps. Are you forgetting all that?'

'I know how brutal the Germans are,' Mother said. 'I know of Hitler's hatred of the Jews. But what good will it do for him to kill innocent civilians? How many Jews can Hitler kill, after all? A thousand, two thousand?'

The arguments, the shouting and the pleading went on and on. But in the end Father conceded to Mother's wishes, and only Luba and I fled our home.

Before we left, my father gave me his golden Longines watch, which had been a wedding gift from his mother-in-law. He told me to take good care of it, because it might save our lives one day.

∗∗∗

'You must have been only fifteen or sixteen then, right?' Moniek said after I had finished relating the story. 'Were you scared?'

'I was dumb at the time. It didn't seem real to me. It was like I thought we were going on an overnight picnic.'

I told him of our escape from Dubno and the early days of running. Although it had happened three years ago, it was still vivid in my mind…

∗∗∗

Luba and I had joined an endless stream of men, women, and children heading east toward the pre-1939 Russian-Polish border some thirty miles from Dubno. We walked amid the cacophony of Messerschmitts overhead and the deafening roar of artillery and not-too-distant German tanks. The roads were clogged with heavy motorized army equipment heading west: tanks on giant carriers, self-propelled artillery with long barrels, armoured cars carrying helmetted soldiers, heavy trucks and other assorted vehicles. There was hardly room for us to walk, and soldiers soon forced us off the paved road.

Outside the town, we walked for days past hills and valleys, fields and forests, while occasional flares in the distance brightened the sky all around us. As we neared the border crossing, we were dismayed to learn that Russian guards were not letting people through.

Luba, never one to take no for an answer, grabbed my hand and forced her way through the crowd of refugees to catch up with a small Soviet army truck. 'Please take us with you,' she called to the soldiers. '*Please!*'

Their eyes examined Luba, and they smiled to each other.

It's the braids, I thought.

'Come on, young comrade,' one of them said, motioning to her.

I sensed the soldiers' disappointment as they saw me join her, but by then we were on the truck, moving slowly through the crowd. Minutes later we were at the border crossing. The army soldiers made humorous remarks to the border guards about the cute young lady and her little brother, and the guards smiled and waved us through.

One of the soldiers turned to us and, in a friendly manner, explained that we should go left to Slavutka, a village a few miles away, where we should be able to find shelter. They had to go in the other direction.

We thanked him and started the trek to Slavutka. There we spent the night in a gym crowded with other refugees who had also found a way to slip through the border.

In the morning, we moved on to the Shepetovka railroad station. Waiting trains filled the station, with some heading west and others, east. Some carried equipment and soldiers to the front, while others overflowed with the wounded, many bandaged head-to-toe and arrayed on stretchers in cattle cars with doors flung open.

People holding bundles and valises, desperate to board a train, overflowed the platform, while rifle-bearing soldiers, roaming amid them, restrained the crowd from jumping onto the tracks.

Luba and I retreated to a small wooded area nearby and launched into a quarrelsome dialogue as to how to proceed. Sentries were stationed at the cabooses of some trains, while others had sentries perched on top of their passenger and freight cars. Our only hope was to jump onto one of the trains heading east, but we feared being shot.

Then a locomotive sounded a whistle. We reacted instinctively, running toward one of the passenger cars. Luck was with us, as the sentries were apparently looking elsewhere.

Luba reached the steps at the head of the train car and pulled herself up. I waited until she was secure and then hoisted myself, while the train was already in motion and gaining speed, onto the steps toward the end of the car.

I moved surreptitiously through the open door and placed myself and my little valise in a corner. Soon, the door closed and we were off, at a snail's pace, going east. I had lost track of Luba, but I knew she was safely in the car.

Among the wounded, a young uniformed soldier lay on his back on the floor along the wall across from me. His neck had been torn open, exposing his trachea, windpipe and part of the chest cavity. Blood spurted out with each pulsing of the heart. He choked as if drowning, trying to breathe. His face was twisted in agony, and his eyes had taken on the sheen of glass. The lips of his half-open mouth tightened as if to scream. He held his hands clenched and his legs stiffly bent at the knees. People had edged away from him and kept their gazes elsewhere.

An orderly with a Red Cross band on his arm approached the wounded soldier. He knelt down, took out his stethoscope, and listened to the soldier's chest. Then he slowly got up, looked around, pulled a revolver out of his back pocket, pressed the muzzle against the soldier's temple, and pulled the trigger. The soldier's legs recoiled convulsively, as if pulled by a puppeteer's string. His body contorted and tightened. The blood flow diminished, and the soldier lay motionless. The orderly glanced around again, then walked away to attend to other wounded.

Through all this, I stood like a statue in the corner, quiet and scared. I had never seen a wounded, bleeding, dying man before, and certainly had never seen anyone be shot to death. Nauseated, I held back from vomiting with all the power I could muster.

***

'That must have been terrifying,' Moniek said sympathetically.

My throat tightened with the memory, and I couldn't reply. After several minutes, I finally regained my composure. 'For the first time, I realized that

Luba and I were caught in the middle of the horrible war and were surrounded by danger. I feared for my life.'

'So what happened next?' asked Moniek anxiously.

I drew a breath and continued the story...

***

After two days of bumpy, stop-and-start travel in the stuffy train compartment, Luba and I had arrived in Kiev. I glimpsed the date on a Soviet newspaper as we passed a stand: It was 1 July 1941. People with bundles on their backs and valises in their hands overflowed the station.

Suddenly everything came to a standstill. Stalin's Georgian-accented voice blared from the station's loudspeakers and filled me with excitement. Stalin exhorted the people of the Soviet Union to fight and, if necessary, set fire to their homes should they be forced to flee. I remember the way he ended his speech: 'Future historians will state that Hitler started the war, but Stalin finished it.'

'Wait here with our bags,' Luba said. 'I'll go fetch some food.'

I became anxious at being apart from her, and to make matters worse, she was gone for what seemed a long time. Eventually, I caught sight of her. She was speaking to a young lieutenant in an animated fashion. I picked up our belongings and rushed over to them. Luba introduced me to Lieutenant Leonid Kaganovich.

He explained that he was about to leave for the front and wanted us to deliver a letter to his parents in Kirovograd. 'It will cheer them up to know that I am well,' he said. He was sure that we'd love his parents once we met them and that they'd be happy to take us in for a while and would treat us like family. He secured a pass for us on the next train to Kirovograd, then bade us farewell.

Toward evening-time, we were knocking at the door of the lieutenant's home.

The lieutenant was right: After the introductions and joy at reading their son's letter, the Kaganoviches had us wash up, eat a simple but filling meal, and helped us settle into their home. In no time at all, they were treating us like their own children. We learned that Mikhail Kaganovich was director of a munitions factory in town and that his wife, Neena, was the high school principal. They explained that Kirovograd was their home, where they were born and raised and where they felt safe.

One morning Neena grabbed Luba and told her that the Germans were fast approaching the city and that we should leave and head further east. They helped us with arrangements for the next train we would board, headed eastward to the town of Voroshilovgrad.

They bade us goodbye and we left. (Hindsight would prove that we had made the right decision to flee: We found our two dear friends in Uzbekistan, the same place where we washed up a year later. The war had indeed caught up with them, and they had become refugees like us.)

A day or so later, in early August 1941, we arrived in Voroshilovgrad, where Luba found a job as a teacher and I enrolled in the high school and delivered mail after hours.

A few months later, the German army caught up with us again. Early one morning, we repeated the drill that we had learned in Shepetovka: We waited at the train station and jumped on the train heading east to Stalingrad.

***

'Stalingrad!' Moniek broke in. 'Were you there in the middle of the fighting?'

'Not quite. I'll tell you about that later.' I explained to him that our stay was brief, and that we left a few days later, after Luba had visited the regional education department and secured a teaching job in Aksai, about fifty miles southwest of Stalingrad. It was October 1941.

I looked at Moniek as we traipsed along. 'Now, before I continue, I want to know more about you.'

He shrugged. 'There isn't much to tell. Your story is more interesting.'

At my urging, he said he had been born and raised in an Orthodox Jewish family in Krakow, in western Poland. He had never finished high school, but he had several patents to his name, including a major one pending to modernize the Polish telephone system. The war had abruptly changed the course of his life.

He and his older brother, Yosef, had left their family and fled east when the Germans invaded Poland in the fall of 1939. They had landed in Lvov, in southeast Poland. In July 1940 the NKVD, Stalin's secret police, picked them up – as they did many of their compatriots – and deported them to a slave labor camp in Siberia.

The conditions there were terrible. As the temperature plummeted to minus thirty degrees Fahrenheit, many of the inmates suffered frozen limbs. Moniek and Yosef wrapped their shoes with newspapers, which kept their feet from freezing.

They were saved from almost certain death when his brother was made the camp's bookkeeper. That assured the brothers an extra portion of bread and provided a place to occasionally warm up. Moniek stated that only a fraction of the seven thousand inmates who had arrived at the camp survived the harsh conditions: the cold winters with hunger and dysentery, and the summers with malaria.

'It was God's will that we live,' Moniek concluded.

'How did you and your brother get out?'

He explained that in the fall of 1941, Stalin released all Polish prisoners. The two brothers left the camp and traveled by train to Samarkand. Yosef found work as a bookkeeper on a collective farm, and Moniek became the maintenance engineer on another farm. Both farms were only a few miles from Samarkand.

'I almost landed in Siberia as well,' I said after he had finished his story. He cast me a quizzical glance. 'How so?'

'Remember, we were sent to Aksai, where Luba was assigned to be a teacher in the local high school? We went there and found a room in a small hovel. It had dirt floors, cracked windows, a small metal stove, a toilet in the corner, a table and chairs, and a few iron beds. We joined two other families. The head of one of them, Mr. Vasily Wiener, ran a tobacco factory in Odessa, which was being evacuated to Stalingrad. We would meet up with him again later. The other couple, in their fifties or so, became ill from cold and malnutrition and soon died, leaving behind their simple-minded son.'

I recounted the events which almost landed *me* in Siberia during the most harrowing time of our whole wartime journey…

***

Winter had come early to Aksai. It was one of the most severe according to the locals, with snowdrifts reaching the roof of our hovel and temperatures plummeting to minus twenty degrees Fahrenheit.

The school gave Luba, as a teacher, some coal, but it didn't last long. Luba and I suffered frost-bitten toes and fingers. Most of the fences around town had already been scavenged by people who used the wood for heat.

One night, venturing outside, I found some loose planks from a neighbouring broken fence. In sheer ecstasy we broke them into pieces and lit a fire in the stove. Unfortunately, it didn't last long.

The next night I searched for more wood, and spotted a tree stump on our neighbour's property lying next to a big pile of timber. As it was too heavy for me to lift, I returned to the hovel and convinced the young disabled man to help me retrieve the heavy and awkward stump. Huffing and puffing, we managed to wrestle it into our room.

Half an hour later, Luba and I were startled by a loud knock on the door. I unlatched it, and a tall policeman stood there, looking grim. 'Which one of you took this?' he demanded, flicking a hand at the stump in the middle of our floor.

'I did,' I told him. My heart was already racing. *Was it illegal to take a stump?*

'Oh no, I helped him with it,' Luba protested. 'It was all my idea.'

'Then you're both under arrest.'

He took us to the police station, where we were immediately separated. I found myself in a small cell that reeked of urine and faeces. A pail in the corner served as the toilet. Two men were stretched out on the earthen floor, snoring under a single blanket. An orderly gave me a blanket and directed me to lie down in the other corner. I wrapped myself in the foul-smelling thing and eventually fell asleep.

A few hours later, a policeman awakened me, took me to a small, well-lit office and ordered me to sit in front of a desk. I fidgeted there for long minutes until a slim, wiry man in a down jacket came in and sat behind the desk. He had gray hair and dark, penetrating eyes.

'Your name?' he said harshly.

'Mikhail Moysieyevicz Kesler,' I replied, trying to keep the fear out of my voice. 'Please, sir, where is my sister?'

He ignored my question. 'Where are you from?'

'Dubno, Poland, sir.' I told him of our travels that had brought us to Aksai.

He peppered me with questions for a long time, wanting to know if my sister and I had any connections in Poland or Russia. Did I have instructions or letters to give to anybody? What other languages did I speak? Did I have any connections with Zionists? It occurred to me that he thought I was a spy.

Then, unexpectedly, he changed the direction of the questioning. 'How much wood did you steal?'

I tried to explain how cold we were and how, in despair, I had hauled in the stump of wood from the next property.

'Did you know it was government property?'

'No, I did not.'

'Are you blind?' he yelled at me. 'Can't you read the sign? That is the town's lumberyard!'

'I didn't see the sign. I'm sorry.'

'How many times have you stolen wood from this property?'

'Just…just this once.'

He sneered and slapped the papers on his desk. 'I have sworn testimony that you stole wood many times before.'

I tried to keep my gaze steady against his hot glare. 'Well…I did pick up two small planks from a broken fence on the other side of our cottage.'

'And what did you do before that? How did you survive the cold without a fire of some sort?'

'We used coal that the school gave us. But it ran out –'

'You're telling me a lot of lies!' he shouted. 'You've been stealing government wood, using some of it for yourself, and selling the rest to other people.'

'I didn't do any such thing, sir.'

'Let's see how your story is a week or a month from now, as you and your sister rot away here.' He got up without another word and stalked out of the room.

The policeman escorted me back to my cell. I had no idea what had become of Luba, and worry about her kept me awake in the cold cell for most of the night.

The next evening, long past midnight, the policeman again took me to the room where I had been interrogated the night before.

The grey-haired officer shuffled his papers and remained quiet for a while. Then he resumed his questioning, at first speaking in a calm, reasonable tone. 'Mikhail, your sister has confessed that you stole a lot of wood from the town's lumberyard. Either she is lying – and if so, she will pay for it dearly – or *you* are lying. Be sure of one thing: Neither your sister nor you will leave this place until you tell us the whole truth.' Now his voice rose until he was bellowing. 'I want to know who your accomplices are. Who have you and your sister been working with to steal all that wood from government property?'

I felt the blood rush to my face. 'I'm telling the whole truth, and I don't believe that my sister confessed to anything else. She's not a liar, and she would not tell things that aren't true.'

My answer enraged him. He stood suddenly, leaned across the desk, and slapped my face with all his force. 'You're accusing me of lying? Do you know what you're doing? You're offending a government official. Such an offence carries heavy punishment!'

My face stung, but I refused to give him the satisfaction of seeing me lift my hand to it. 'Sir, I don't mean to offend you, but I know my sister.'

'Well, well, you're a stubborn young man, aren't you? We shall see what the truth is.'

He stormed out of the room, and the silent policeman took me back to my cell. I lay on the floor, trembling with fear.

Around midnight on the third night, I again faced my inquisitor.

'I have prepared a summary of my interviews with you.' He flung a sheaf of papers across the desk at me. 'Sign it.'

With sleepy, bleary eyes, I leafed through pages of things that I had never said, among them a confession that I stole, on numerous occasions, large quantities of government property.

'Sign it,' he commanded, 'and I'll let you go.'

I considered my options for a moment, then said, 'If I sign this, will you let my sister go?'

'Yes.'

I felt I had no choice, and I signed the document.

I was released the next morning. I returned to our hovel and found Luba there crying.

'I've worried about you so much,' she sobbed, clinging to me.

The grey-haired officer had lied. Luba had been released immediately after our arrest and had certainly never confessed to anything.

✱✱✱

'Did you find out who told the police that you had stolen wood?' Moniek asked.

I nodded. 'The woman next door, who had submitted the affidavit of my alleged crime, turned out to be an important Communist Party official. She was in charge of the lumberyard and was, in fact, peddling its goods on the side. The charges she made against me were false but surely could have landed me in Siberia.'

'I'm surprised you weren't sent there, since you signed the confession.'

'Luckily, a Jewish lawyer from Stalingrad had come to Aksai to defend an important case. Luba learned of him and begged him to defend me, and he agreed. The trial resulted in a mild sentence of six months' probation, thanks to him. Finally, Luba and I could breathe easily.'

'Thank God for that,' Moniek said. 'What did you do next?'

'I went back to school and took a course to be a veterinary assistant, which I completed in June 1942. Meanwhile, a huge German army began to encircle Stalingrad. Our hope was that we could run ahead of the moving armies to Stalingrad, cross the Volga, and move farther east. So one night we packed up our belongings and stealthily left Aksai on a train.'

'To Stalingrad?' Moniek said.

'Yes, in mid-July 1942, smack dab in the middle of the siege and one of the biggest battles of the war!...'

✱✱✱

I could hardly recognize the city. It was half-devastated from when I was there last, nearly a year earlier, before spending the winter in Aksai. Military traffic clogged the streets, and soldiers crowded each corner. I could sense an air of crisis gripping the city. As the night wore on, the shriek of artillery shells, the roar of aircraft bombardment, the hiss of anti-aircraft fire bursting in the air, and the wail of sirens of the emergency vehicles continued unabated. Flares lit up the sky, as if it were broad daylight. The terror of the night made me fear that the world around me would soon be aflame and engulf me.

***

'How did you get out of there alive?' Moniek asked.

'It was my father's watch.' I told him about the Longines watch my father had given to me, and his admonition that it could save our life – which was exactly what happened.

Moniek cast me a sideways glance. 'You used it as a bribe?'

'Not exactly...'

***

We had heard that a ship, the *Astrakhan*, docked at the nearby Volga River, was to leave for the Caspian Sea. Luba and I decided to book passage, so I went to the dock and joined a long queue of people waiting to buy tickets.

Hours went by as the line crawled. The July sun was hot and dizzying. I felt as if I were being carried along by the surging crowd. Sweaty, thirsty and tired, I closed my eyes against the relentless sun and fell into a kind of stupor.

Suddenly, I felt a violent jerk and the tearing of my shirt pocket. I opened my eyes and saw a teenaged boy running away. I reached for my Longines watch in the shirt pocket, but it was gone.

I jumped out of the queue and began chasing the teenager, but he was fast, far quicker than I. He melted into the crowd, nowhere to be found.

I despaired. The watch was the most valuable possession Luba and I had. It was the last thing Father had given me when we parted, and his words rang in my ears. 'Take good care of this watch, Mekhel. It may save your life one day.' Now I had lost it. I felt angry, bitter and disappointed with myself.

There was no way to rejoin the queue, now blocked off by policemen. Luba and I had lost our chance to leave Stalingrad.

The next morning, we learned that the *Astrakhan* had hit a mine. Everyone – all those men, women, and children who had been with me in that queue at the dock – had drowned.

***

'It was God's will that you live,' Moniek said after I had finished. 'You should recite the *Gomel* blessing.'

The *Gomel* blessing was traditionally recited by Jews saved by God from life-threatening danger. But I had a different view. 'I believe it was my father's blessings that brought about the miracle.'

He nodded thoughtfully.

'We stayed in Stalingrad with Mr. Wiener and his family, whom we had first met in Aksai. After a week or so, Mr. Wiener was able to secure a decent rowboat with two strong young rowers who brought us at night to the eastern Volga shore. We were able to catch a train to the nearest rail junction, where we caught another train going to Tashkent, Uzbekistan. There, Luba got a permit to teach, and I to practice as a veterinarian, in Syr Darya, near the Kyrgyzstan border. We arrived in our new home in early September 1942. 'For the next couple of years we lived among the Uzbeks. That's where we were when Luba almost died...'

***

A year into our stay in Syr Darya, typhoid fever spread like wildfire. One morning in early September 1943, Luba awoke hot and perspiring. Her fever soon shot up to the point where she became delirious. A friend helped me to get a horse and wagon from the farm, and we took Luba to the hospital. I stayed with her until a kind doctor assured me that she would be all right.

I had to visit the farms, and when I returned to the hospital three days later, Luba's fever had spiked again. This time the doctor, concerned, advised me to stay close by for the next few days. I stayed with my horse in a little park adjoining the hospital, where I slept on one of the benches for the next two nights. I was afraid that Luba might die.

From Lviv, Ukraine to Samarkand, Uzbekistan: approximately 3,000 miles

Map data ©2016

When I came to fetch her with a horse and wagon, I could hardly recognize her. She looked like a skeleton, her eyes sunken and motionless.

'You're a good brother,' the doctor said. 'You'll need to continue being good to her. The illness has affected her mind, as typhoid fever does sometimes. I hope she'll pull out of that difficulty, but she'll need a lot of loving care.'

I took Luba home and put her gently to bed. I fetched a chicken from the farm and prepared a meal Mother used to make – chicken soup with potatoes, carrots and other vegetables. But Luba would not eat. Furthermore, she would not speak to me; she seemed unable to utter a word.

I tried a different tack, cooking the chicken in the soup until the meat was tender. I tore the chicken into small pieces and mashed the contents of the pot with a fork until they became almost liquid. I poured some of the liquid into a glass and fed it slowly to Luba. She liked it, and this became her diet, in small quantities.

Slowly, she began to eat some soft vegetables, and then pieces of meat. But she remained speechless and unresponsive. I cajoled her, begged her to talk to me, told her funny stories and reminded her of us playing as children, at home. She listened with vacant eyes, staring into the distance without uttering a word.

'Luba, Lubushka, wake up,' I pleaded with her.

Nothing.

I bathed her with water warmed on the grill, and tended to all her needs. I felt a deep, overwhelming love for her, mixed with worry and despair. In the night's quietude, I recited psalms that I remembered, and spoke to my parents, begging for their help.

Weeks passed, and I began to think that Luba would never recover. The thought of losing my sister terrified me. Our relationship during the past few years had become symbiotic. I felt I could not live without her – without her will to live and to fight, without her ingenuity to survive amidst the chaos of the war.

One morning, nearly a month since Luba had fallen ill, I woke up reflecting about my home. It was the time of the year when we celebrated Rosh Hashono, Jewish New Year. I remembered Mother, Father, Luba and I sitting around the festive table and Father praising the way I chanted my solo at the Great Synagogue: *Haben Yakir Li Efrayim* ('I will remember my dear son, Ephrayim, said the Lord').

I began humming the tune. Then, seeing Luba stir, I sang louder, enunciating clearly each word, and chanting each note with all the care and beauty I could muster. Suddenly, Luba started singing along with me, tentatively at first, then more confidently as we went on.

'Luba, Lubushka, you sing so beautifully.' I embraced her and covered her face with gentle kisses. 'You'll be all right now!' I exclaimed with tears in my eyes.

✳✳✳

'Blessed be God, the healer of us all,' Moniek murmured.

We reached the large barn where Moniek stayed. His corner room, with a little window barely large enough to admit sunlight, contained a small table and a single cot. He told me that I would sleep on blankets on the dirt floor next to the cot.

He sighed with relief as he put down his heavy backpack. 'The tuna fish cans are what made the load so heavy,' he noted.

A few moments later, we sat at the rickety table beside the small window. Moniek took a black yarmulke from the backpack and put it on to cover his head as he recited the blessing before the meal. Then he fetched a can-opener from the table's drawer and pried open a can of tuna fish. He emptied it into an earthenware bowl, gave me a flatbread, and I joined him for supper.

He told me that the tuna fish was his main source of protein and would be mine as well while I worked with him on the farm. He urged me to eat all of my share, since this was the only major daytime meal we would have. The rest of the day we'd have to make do with fresh vegetables that we would find on the farm.

Moniek's strictness with food impressed me. He was an Orthodox Jew and adhered to the traditions and rabbinic guidelines on diet and the minutiae of day-to-day life. As we ate, he pointed out his belief that his respect for tradition and strong faith in God had seen him through his horrible experiences in Siberia. They had also helped him to feel proud as a Jew among strangers.

He looked at me with a zeal that alerted me to the strength of his convictions and will. His eyes, which darkened as the sun descended, probed me and made me a bit uncomfortable. I knew he was wondering about the depth of my convictions. In truth, I hadn't been an observant Jew since leaving home three years earlier. My sister and I had been constantly on the run or living in small villages among Uzbeks. We'd had practically no exposure to other Jews. We did not observe the Jewish holidays, since we didn't even know exactly when they took place.

Besides, we had come from a liberal, traditional home, with the emphasis on *liberal*. Our mother had a much more progressive background than our father. Her own father had died of tuberculosis in his forties and had left behind a young widow with four daughters and two sons. Her brother Mekhel, my namesake, had been a socialist leader and his philosophy permeated their household.

Would I be able to satisfy Moniek by becoming more religious? I wasn't sure. I'd had enough authoritarian life under Stalin. I didn't need more of that in my daily life.

Moniek took my silence as a cue. He changed topics and began to talk about the next day's work. He explained that his job was to keep the farm machinery in good working order. He did it mostly by finding replacement parts in abandoned equipment and adapting them to repair the disabled units. My task would be to locate spare parts.

After finishing our meal, we got up from the table. Moniek gave me some sheets to cover myself with and we went to sleep.

We rose at dawn to a busy day.

My job proved to be more interesting and difficult than Moniek had described it. I had to work from morning till evening, unearthing abandoned equipment in fields overgrown with weeds. This challenged my knack for mechanics and my ability to visualize how to adapt and modify parts from older machinery for later models.

Sometimes I needed to second-guess Moniek's needs for a particular part, and when I mistook them, I discovered that Moniek had a short fuse. He'd burst out angrily on such occasions and harshly criticize my stupidity. Each time this happened, it would take a couple of days for his anger to subside.

Fear and tension visited me daily, accompanied by scary dreams at night. But this happened less often as the days went by. The intensity of my work and the fresh air did their job.

Moniek would go to Samarkand on weekends to spend the Sabbath with his friends. In early June 1944 he got permission to spend a couple of days to celebrate Shavuot (Pentecost, or 'The Feast of Weeks'). Upon his return, the office secretary, a beautiful young Uzbek woman, came out to greet Moniek and to shake his hand. I noticed that he was reluctant to do so, feebly acknowledging her advances with a smile. This, too, exemplified his disciplined observance of the Orthodox rabbis' precepts. Young Jewish men were to keep their distance from young women until engagement.

Seeing this also reminded me of my own encounters with a somewhat younger Uzbek woman. I had met Mahdu the first time I ventured to the Uzbek farms with the chief veterinarian of the area as his assistant. She was the daughter of the richest farmer and beautiful, with long braids and dark eyes. She'd often stop by to chat with me at my temporary home, where I stayed with one of the farmer's families. She would tell me enthusiastically about her plans to attend high school in Samarkand, where her uncle was a supervisor. She was studying Russian and other high school subjects with an itinerant instructor.

The thought teased my mind that maybe one day we might meet in Samarkand.

∗∗∗

One Sunday, Moniek returned from Samarkand with great news. On 6 June 1944, the Western Allies – mainly the United States and Great Britain – had invaded Normandy with their Expeditionary Force under the leadership of General Dwight D. Eisenhower.

I devoured the news in *Izvestia*, the Soviet government newspaper, which Moniek brought with him. The Western Allies had landed in Normandy and suffered enormous casualties. Articles and editorials expressed great relief that the Western Allies had finally kept their word and had begun to relieve the Soviet Union's onerous burden of fighting Hitler alone for the past three years.

Moniek also hinted that he had spent some time with Luba, whom he had seen on several earlier occasions in Samarkand. That pricked my ears. *Moniek is cozying up to Luba. My, my! Am I going to become a shadchan (matchmaker)?* That filled me with joy. But then a few alarm bells sounded. *Would I soon lose my only friend from the past three years?* 'Crazy wings of fate,' I murmured.

***

In late June, Tartar refugees began arriving by the truckload. These poor, frightened and despondent people recounted to me how they had been torn from their homes in the middle of the night and deported from the Crimea by the Soviet secret police. They had been accused of collaborating with the Germans. They also told me that many of their relatives and friends had been deported to labour camps in Siberia.

Not long after my encounter with the Tartars, Moniek and I had a conversation following one of his visits to Samarkand.

His response to my account of the Tartars' ordeal was eye-opening. 'What else is new?' he said, and shrugged his shoulders.

That provoked a short, tense exchange between us.

He continued with an update of the unsettling situation he had found in Samarkand. 'The city is flooded with refugees, mostly Jewish. Some of them are from where we fled, but many come from western Ukraine.'

I listened intently.

'When I go to the city on the Sabbath, I pray and rest, but I also meet and talk to people there. The stories I hear are even more painful than the one you told me. Invariably, they tell of families being separated and punished for mere hearsay. Jews are like telegraph posts. They convey information. One thing they have in common is that they all tell of brutalities of the regime. They speak quietly and say that Stalin is just a little bit better than Hitler, that he uses Siberia instead of crematories to dispose of anybody he suspects of disloyalty.'

I must have looked stunned, because Moniek paused for a moment so that I could take in all that he was saying.

'Have you heard of *Darkness at Noon*, the book by Arthur Koestler, the Hungarian-Jewish historian and philosopher? It tells of the hundreds of innocent Jewish writers and poets whom Stalin falsely accused of trumped-up crimes. He would jail them, send them to Siberia, or take them out and shoot them.'

'So is there any hope for us here?' I exclaimed in horror.

'I have heard rumours from Jewish friends that I know well and feel I can trust. They tell me that the Allies have begun setting up "displaced persons camps" in the liberated territories that they have occupied. Our best hope is for the war to end and for us to reach one of those camps and from there go to Palestine.'

That filled me with excitement. *Maybe we'll be able to leave after all!*

2

The Weaver

In early July 1944 Moniek took me back to Luba, who had moved, in the meantime, to a different location. Our new quarters, a sublet from a couple in their sixties by the name of Zuckerman, consisted of a portion of a common hallway. A curtain separated our assigned place from a coal stove, a sink and a broken-up storage area. Another curtain opened into the common 'outhouse' – little more than a hole in the ground.

'Make yourself comfortable in our new palatial suite,' Luba said sarcastically.

'I knew you could do it, Luba.' I embraced her. 'You're terrific.'

What would have crushed my spirit three years earlier, I took in stride. My encounters with death during the intervening years had taught me just how adaptable I could be.

Luba saw Moniek off with a warm smile and blushing cheeks, and he left wearing what seemed to me a glowing expression.

'This is where we'll have to stay until we get rich,' Luba declared, then burst out laughing. She told me that she had made arrangements with the Zuckermans to hire me as a weaver once I learned how to use a loom.

While I was working beside Moniek at his collective farm, Luba had gotten to know the Zuckermans through her new network of friends. She rented a small part of the rundown shack the Zuckermans had found several years earlier in the old city. Esther Zuckerman, a short, slim woman with dark hair and eyes, resembled our mother, which drew us closer to her. Being childless, Esther became fond of Luba and treated her like the daughter she never had. I, too, became a member of their extended family.

Rabbi Issachar Zuckerman and his wife had prudently left their home in Bessarabia, part of Romania, ahead of the German army's conquests in June 1941. They made their way to Samarkand with the help of Esther's cousin, Aaron, a textile manufacturer who had fled Lodz in 1941. Aaron was an expert weaver on handlooms, and after his arrival, he gradually established a cottage industry weaving and selling cloth to the local population, who used it in their colourful garb. He set up his cousins in the business, finding a loom and a young apprentice to help out. They were eager to introduce us to the business and arranged for me to learn the trade at Aaron's workshop.

During the next few weeks, I was Aaron's apprentice, learning on one of his looms, and then he placed me at the Zuckermans', on their newly-acquired second loom.

A few months later, Luba and I decided to buy a loom of our own with the Zuckermans' blessing, but we needed money to do it. Luba suggested that we ask for the help of Osher Balaban, her classmate from Dubno who had become a bigwig in Samarkand's municipal government. Osher had issued the fake passport that allowed me to live in the open. She said he had been a good friend to her, and that I had nothing to fear.

The first words Osher uttered when Luba and I met him in his office were in Yiddish: '*Vosmachtu, Mikele* (my diminutive Yiddish name) – How are you?'

He had aged, I noticed, and had quite a bit of grey in his dark hair. He towered over the two of us – tall and slender, with dark eyes and a broad smile. We sat, and I told him that I remembered him well and also his father, who had taught history at my Hebrew school. The conversation drifted to our escape from Dubno – the very same day he and his brother had fled. No, his travels all the way to Samarkand did not take the same path, but yes, he had stopped over in Stalingrad in July 1942, just as we had. Being five or six years older, he was drafted into the Soviet army and was badly wounded.

'You see my twisted left arm?' he said, showing me. 'But that had its good part as well. That's how I met Zhenya, who worked as a nurse in the hospital where I was treated, and we've been together ever since.'

I thanked him profusely for helping Luba save my life. I wanted to go on, but he put an index finger to his lips and I stopped. He continued, telling us that in Samarkand there were thousands of Jews who had escaped ahead of the German army, from Dubno and other places, and that they all tried to be helpful to one another here.

The conversation shifted to our present circumstances, and Luba described our luck in finding the Zuckermans, how they'd introduced me to cloth weaving, arranged for my training and work in their small shop, and our plans to become independent weavers. When Luba inquired about how we might approach people in Samarkand to get our own loom, Osher offered instead to trust us with a modest loan so that we could go ahead and start doing business.

'I'm sure you'll do well and soon be able to repay me.'

We expressed our gratitude and left.

A few days later, we found a second-hand loom, and Luba and I became entrepreneurs. I would weave, and she would sell the colourful cloth I produced on the black market – the only market available for private exchange of goods in the Soviet Union. We were now owners of a money-generating machine. The back-breaking work kept me occupied from dawn till dusk. But it felt good to be able to feed Luba and myself and still put aside a few roubles for travel at war's end.

The Weaver

© Copyright February 2008, Don Bloom, E. Brunswick, NJ.

Slowly, I regained my confidence and felt a sense of pride that we'd been able to establish some independence and security in such an insecure place. As 1945 dawned, we started dreaming of returning to Poland, and then going with our parents to Palestine to build a new home.

3

Grow Up!

The year 1945 proved memorable for Luba and me. Our budding enterprise helped us along. Sensing the war's end, we also began preparing to return home, although we had no way of knowing if anything remained there.

***

We welcomed 1945 with a small feast. Luba had brought home a fish, a rare delicacy for us. When she returned from the market, I stopped shuffling the loom's shuttle and stepped into the hall to greet my sister, whose lips and cheeks formed a familiar, mischievous smile.

'So you did it again,' I said. 'Which NKVD man did you have to pay off this time?'

'Never you mind.' Her eyes, sparkling with excitement, reflected the descending sun. 'I simply bartered your cloth for a well-deserved meal, so sit down, and let's enjoy our small celebration before you run off to school.'

I reminded Luba that the institute was closed for New Year's.

As we were eating, Moniek appeared. He, too, had the day off and wanted to spend some time with us. The head of the farm where he worked, a devout Muslim, allowed him to take off for the Sabbath and holidays, and Moniek always visited Luba on those occasions.

The pair had grown closer since they'd met the previous fall. In Moniek's presence, Luba became much more animated and vivacious, with a bounce in her step and a bell-like ring in her voice. My sister was falling in love. Her neatly-groomed braids had grown back to the length of a year and a half earlier, before her near-fatal bout with typhoid. She absently played with them as Moniek joined us at the table.

'How did it go today, Luba?' he asked.

'*Veni, vidi, vici* – I came, I saw, and I conquered,' Luba replied, and recounted her adventure at the market.

Moniek expressed concern that the NKVD could arrest her. 'It's a strange country we live in. It's all right to starve to death, but it's a crime to make and sell for simple necessities.'

'I don't have much choice, do I?'

'Maybe soon you will,' Moniek replied. 'It looks like good news is on the way.'

He explained that the Red Army had reached Poland's western border and was poised to move into Germany. A few weeks before, they had liberated Krakow, his hometown, and he had written home. He was expecting to hear from someone in the family any day. In the west the American and British forces under Eisenhower had liberated most of France and were entering the Benelux countries. In the south, the American and British armies, under Generals Patton and Montgomery, were forging through Italy and Greece and approaching central Europe. He tempered his enthusiasm with rumours from his Jewish friends that Eisenhower's forces had encountered sudden, stiff resistance from a reinforced German army in Belgium. He expressed his hope that God would help to resolve that situation before long.

Luba sighed, stating that her letters sent home had come back marked *Address unknown*. The Red Army had taken over Dubno earlier that year, and her inability to reach our parents worried her. Talking of our home brought tears to her eyes.

Moniek went to her and embraced her gently. 'Come, take a walk with me.'

'Meanwhile,' I said, pushing away from the table, 'I need to make my quota of material for Luba to barter tomorrow, lest I be fired.'

I returned to my cramped cubicle filled with the loom and its accessories. Hot in the summer and cold in the winter, it was my personal shell and my personal hell. From this small space, I wove the cloth that secured bread and the basic essentials for our survival. I spent nearly all my waking hours in solitude, tugging a pulley that sent a mouse-like shuttle across the loom table and lay one strand after another to produce inches, then feet, then yards of colourful cloth. As the shuttle flew back and forth, it evoked images of trains rushing rhythmically along their tracks, *one-two-three, one-two-three...*

I sighed, recalling the blessed trains that had taken Luba and me from one end of the world to the other, from our home some three thousand miles away, through the wilderness of the steppes, to this tiny haven in a strange, exotic place. Other recollections flashed through my mind: the jail in Aksai, where I landed for stealing a stump of wood to heat our frozen hut; the unbelievable happenstance of the stolen Longines watch, which my father had given me, saving our lives in Stalingrad; Luba's heroic feat to yank me out of the Soviet army.

I couldn't have survived those ordeals without Luba, who, though only a few years older, was much more streetwise and clever. Barely five feet tall and slender, she had fearlessly fought off sexual advances and corrupt government agents as we moved from one place to the next. Her constitution was surprisingly strong, given a childhood battle with tuberculosis and her more recent bout with typhoid. Luba's energy, enthusiasm and relentless will to live lifted me through the many dangers we had faced. She was my best friend, and, during the past four and a half years, my *only* friend. But now her loyalty extended to Moniek, who had become like an older brother to me.

Am I about to lose her? Will the end of the war and changing circumstances cause them to drift away from me?

Barely twenty years old, I felt lost and lonely, cast adrift on a still-stormy ocean. Time had bestowed good fortune on Luba. She was in love and soon to marry, I presumed.

A chill traversed my bones then, suddenly, a voice within me offered counsel: *It's time to stand on your own two feet. Grow up!*

4

The Student

In September 1944 I had signed up to attend evening school at the Uzbek Economic Institute, which offered training programmes for young men and women, designed specifically to meet the war's needs. My evening walks after a long day's work, from the squalor of the old city to the refreshing elegance of the new one, filled me with relief.

I was surprised to find that the majority of students were women. Most of the men were off fighting at the front. Soon I began to feel special as the female students, and even the young instructors, seemed to dote on me. That privileged feeling calmed my fears of being put on the defensive and recognized as a deserter. Further, I discovered that I was equipped to take a double course load so I could finish the two-year programme in one year.

***

A day after the New Year's holiday, I walked briskly to the institute. Cold weather had descended on Samarkand, taxing the last reserves of energy and bringing much illness. The poverty that inundated the old city took a particularly heavy toll on the poor and the sick at this time of year. As I navigated the narrow streets, I came across an emaciated corpse stretched out on the steps of a building. This lifeless body, inches from where I stood, sent shockwaves through me, and a terrifying thought rose in my mind: *Are my parents still alive or had they, God forbid, suffered the same fate as this man?* I had read in the papers that the Germans starved ghetto inmates before dragging them out to be killed in the nearby woods.

I quickened my pace to distance myself from the gruesome sight and shake off my dark thoughts. But the image of the corpse remained with me, prompting me to ponder: *Was it luck or pluck that let me and Luba survive while many, like this man, have died?*

Certainly we owed our lives mostly to good luck, to being in the right place at the right time. But a measure of pluck fuelled our good fortune as well, I reflected. Our ability to adapt quickly to the brutal reality had enabled me to become a veterinary assistant and, at seventeen, gain the respect of the farmers in Syr Darya. I had mastered the trade of weaving cloth and was able to feed Luba and myself. Luba, who had gained the friendship and respect of many along the way, possessed a sixth sense for avoiding trouble. We had studied hard and worked hard, while staying alert to dangers, as well as opportunities.

I reached the city's new section, where most of the Russian administrators and my professors lived. The mausoleum of Turko-Mongol conqueror Tamerlane, situated close to the river, appeared abandoned at this late hour. Yet, the shiny blue colours of its world-famous mosaic shone through the descending darkness, as bright and vibrant as if freshly painted, even though it was five hundred years old.

My heart pumping, I approached the two-storey building of the institute and entered the library. Rabbi Zuckerman, an avid radio fan, including shortwave, had told me of startling reports of Eisenhower's forces fighting against great odds in Belgium. *Will I find anything in the press to confirm this?* I wondered.

I picked up the official Communist Party newspaper, *Pravda*, stunned by an article on the front page describing a fierce battle in Belgium that could jeopardize the very existence of the Western forces. I feverishly pieced together news of the setback for Eisenhower and his troops in the forests of Ardennes, spanning parts of Belgium, France and Luxembourg.

In my current events class later that evening, I ventured a brief summary of what I had read in the newspapers about the battle raging in Belgium.

Over the next few weeks, these developments generated much heated discussion in class. Our instructor pointedly questioned whether Eisenhower's Expeditionary Force was prepared to fight the well-tested German war machine. Several of my classmates expressed concerns about whether the West was committed to the enormous sacrifice that an invasion of Germany-proper would demand.

As the Red Army moved inexorably west toward the German capital in the face of formidable resistance, a terrible thought crossed my mind: *What if the Russians roll on, defeat the Germans, and come face-to-face with Eisenhower's forces? Will the latter leave under pressure and return to America?* I worried. *Will I ever be free of this oppressive life under Stalin's iron fist?*

Meanwhile, other news began to crowd my extra-curricular schedule. A meeting was to take place at Yalta in Crimea between the three leaders of the Grand Alliance: Franklin D. Roosevelt, Winston Churchill and Joseph Stalin.

A few weeks after the battle at Ardennes, accounts of the Yalta Conference and its participants began to fill the daily Soviet newspapers. In a show of goodwill, the Soviet government permitted foreign correspondents into the conference and allowed their select observations and accounts to appear in the Soviet press.

Starry-eyed, I gobbled up these reports, sensing that the conference's agreements would have a critical post-war effect on the countries and peoples of Europe. It would surely dictate my and Luba's ability to return home or perhaps travel to Palestine. The news also intrigued me from a human-interest viewpoint. The press and the published sources covering the conference revealed fascinating portraits of the three leaders – Roosevelt, Churchill and, particularly, Stalin – and their interactions. The instructor showed the class an official portrait of the three heads of state, with Roosevelt looking fragile, Churchill stodgy and Stalin, in contrast, vigorous and animated.

The conference opened with much fanfare, and the Soviet press enthusiastically proclaimed successful conclusions of each major item of negotiation. My friend Rabbi Zuckerman, however, heard contrary opinions on his radio by prominent British commentators, and he reported them to me with a mischievous twinkle in his eye. He claimed that Roosevelt had conceded many advantages to Stalin, such as Poland's boundaries, Poland's new government and the basis for choosing new governments in other Red Army-conquered countries.

The seven-day conference ended as it began, with the expectant victors consuming much caviar and offering many flattering toasts. The final communiqués artfully camouflaged the developing cracks in the alliance, which one could read between the lines of news reports in the foreign papers.

Roosevelt and Churchill separately detoured on their journeys back in order to visit the oil-rich monarchies of the Middle East. For the next few days, the newspapers in the library fascinated me with stories and pictures of immense, cheering crowds greeting the two leaders.

5

An Encounter with Mahdu

The end of March 1945 brought balmy weather, more food and shorter bread lines in Samarkand. In a park of the new city that I crossed on my way to the institute, members of an Uzbek opera company performed Verdi's *Otello* in the open air. People shed their winter parkas and sat on benches or on the grass, listening to the trained voices soar above the small orchestra. In the plaza across from the institute, students milled about, spreading the good news: The Red Army had victoriously pushed the Germans westward and was about to enter Vienna!

As I was approaching the institute's main building, I heard a familiar voice. 'Meesha, Meesha.'

I turned around as Mahdu ran over to embrace me.

'What a miracle to find you here!' she exclaimed.

'What are *you* doing here?' I asked.

'Come, let's sit down where it's quiet, and I'll tell you.'

As I looked at Mahdu, a soft sweetness warmed my body. She had matured into a stunningly beautiful young woman. Her dark eyes glowed with excitement, and her sensuous, full red lips almost begged me to kiss her. I extended a hand and she eagerly took it. Hers felt hot and trembled with excitement. She told me that she had come to Samarkand two years earlier to attend the elite gymnasium (which in Europe meant high school), open to children of Soviet administrators and workers. Her uncle headed the gymnasium and had had no difficulty enrolling her. She was about to finish and planned to study nursing at the institute in September. She wanted to help the many wounded soldiers returning from the front. To my question of what she would be doing that summer, she answered that she was planning to take some courses and also visit her family in Syr Darya. 'Meanwhile,' she said with a smile, 'I'll be living with my uncle in Samarkand.'

When she asked how I had disappeared and where to, I stretched the truth nearly to its breaking point, describing my induction into the Soviet army and my subsequent release a few months later, due to pneumonia that had almost killed me. 'I haven't been on the farm for nearly two years,' I said. 'How are your family and Sarrat, who was like a mother to me?'

She assured me that everyone was doing fine and that they often recalled me as the *Bolasi*, or 'boy doctor', of whom they'd all become so fond.

I reminded her how we'd met when I'd been accompanying Dr. Mahmoud, noting how she had blushed when her father introduced us.

'I guess I liked you at first sight.' She laughed. 'And I still like you, even though you disappeared.' With a wink, she added, 'I'll make sure you don't disappear again.'

After agreeing to meet up in a few days, we embraced and then parted.

Over the following weeks we met often, usually at dusk while on my way to classes. I began to look forward to seeing Mahdu, who possessed a sharp, inquisitive mind. I found it surprisingly easy to talk to her and even shared my hope of becoming a scientist or an engineer. She assured me that her father had plenty of money, and that he would help me to achieve my goals.

Mahdu inquired about my parents and my sister. She thought Luba a brave woman and was eager to meet her. I sidestepped her requests for fear of jeopardizing our relationship, since Luba would surely disclose that we were Jewish, and I was unsure how Mahdu would react to that news.

On another occasion, Mahdu wondered whether I'd like to go home with her to the farms to see her father and the friends I had left there nearly two years earlier. I declined and, when she persisted, I told her of the unpleasant conflict I had experienced there two years earlier, when her father and the farmers made me sign a false statement that sheep were missing due to illness, while selling the sheep on the market.

'Dr. Mahmoud threatened to fire me for it,' I said.

Her face reddened. 'Meesha, you do not know the true situation. The Russians were stealing the farmers' property, not the other way around.'

I stared at her, incredulous. 'Dr. Mahmoud made me believe he was a saint.'

'Did you see his mansion?' she asked, her voice rising. 'A few miles from Syr Darya? He lives there with his family, like a prince. Where do you think he gets the means to do that?'

Mahdu's outburst opened my eyes to the widespread corruption among Uzbek farmers and officials. It also showed Mahdu to be shrewd and very capable of defending herself.

My fondness and respect for her began to grow.

Toward the end of May, she returned home for a few weeks. Her absence left a profound void in my evenings. My infatuation with Mahdu, albeit devoid of sexual contact, brought much tumult with it. I feared becoming trapped, torn away from my people and my faith.

6

The Death of a President and the Ascension of a New President

Late on 12 April, Radio Moscow broadcast that President Franklin Delano Roosevelt had died. The news stunned me. I considered Roosevelt our saviour, the architect of the alliance that was saving us from Hitler. As such, I had a profound respect for him. Rabbi Zuckerman and Moniek fanned that respect – and even love for the man – as did, it seemed, the entire Jewish community of Samarkand. I'd set my hopes on Roosevelt's ability to set us free, so that we might return to our homes, or perhaps even leave the blood-soaked continent of Europe for Palestine or America.

Later that same day, Vice President Harry S. Truman was sworn in as the next president of the country, still at war. As I skimmed various newspaper and magazine articles, I learned that Truman, though ill-prepared for the job, appeared to be a quick study.

7

Preparing to Leave

A number of signs appeared in the spring of 1945, signalling the approaching end of the war. In early May the Soviet news agency, TASS, reported that Hitler had committed suicide. A few days later, the senior military command of the German forces offered to surrender. Martial music dominated the Radio Moscow programmes.

On the evening of 8 May I returned home from the institute to find Rabbi Zuckerman and Esther engaged in animated discussion with Luba. Shortly thereafter, Moniek arrived bearing a remarkable letter from his mother, who had survived the war and eagerly awaited her sons' return. Sadly, Moniek's father had perished at Mauthausen. The discussion took an urgent turn when Moniek posed the question of how he might get from Samarkand to Krakow.

'It's more than three thousand miles away,' he said.

'This country is one huge jail!' Rabbi Zuckerman proclaimed from his seat at the table beside his wife. 'You're born here and you die here, and there's no way to leave it.' He recounted his own bitter experience a few months earlier, when he and Esther attempted to return to their home in Romania, which the Red Army had liberated from the Germans.

'Obtaining a permit to travel proved impossible, I'm afraid,' Esther said.

The rabbi nodded. 'And what's to stop Stalin from taking the reins of the Polish government and turning that country into another satellite prison?'

I ventured that ultimately Stalin might realize the advantages of letting people from other lands, who had spent the war years in the Soviet Union, return to their homes. They might then help their compatriots adapt to the Communist regimes.

The rabbi stared up at me through thick glasses, his already large eyes bulging. 'What – you're a goodwill ambassador for this monstrous government now?' He sounded like an angry prophet of Israel.

'Where else would we have survived?' I shot back.

Rabbi Zuckerman's diminutive form quivered as he described the miserable fate of millions of Ukrainian farmers whom Stalin had dispersed, many of them shipped off to Siberia – where most died of cold, starvation and disease – or starved to death on their own farms. Meanwhile, the farms went fallow as famine engulfed Ukraine, the breadbasket of Europe.

I countered that Stalin had mechanized agriculture, turning the Soviet Union into an industrial giant.

'And you know how he did it?' The rabbi was on his feet now, pulling together his long, tattered black coat. 'By starving the people. That's how he saved resources to industrialize the country.' After berating me for believing the sanitized history and for not knowing what was really going on, he turned to Moniek. 'Tell him. Tell him how it was for you.'

Moniek recounted to me his bitter years in Siberia, where most died, if not from hunger and illness, then from exposure. He again mentioned *Darkness at Noon*, explaining that the book told of the fake trials Stalin had arranged to get rid of Jewish poets and other writers, intellectuals, and professionals.

'And does Koestler tell you the rest about Stalin's killing orgy?' Rabbi Zuckerman said. 'Just before the war, he got rid of millions of intelligentsia and high-level government workers, many of them Jewish, by sending them to the coldest parts of Siberia to freeze to death or be executed. No trials, real or fake, just kill, kill, kill!'

Luba cleared her throat. 'Rabbi,' she said in a tactful attempt to cut short his rant, 'do you have any ideas about how Moniek might get back home?'

The rabbi sighed and lowered himself back into the chair. 'Patience and hope. We have lived on hope of redemption for millennia, so we can wait until things settle down. Maybe America will bring Stalin to his senses. Who knows?'

'I'll talk to my friend Osher,' Luba said. 'He helped me get settled here. I trust he'll know what to do.' She smiled up at Moniek. 'We must leave, and we'll find a way.'

8

Worries and Reprieve

Luba's bold pronouncement that Osher Balaban would help us find a way to leave and go home did little to ease my anxiety of what the next day would bring. Memories of Mom and Dad in the late 1930s, discussing in hushed voices Jewish news articles about the gathering dark clouds of war flashed through my mind. The war had ended, at least in Europe. But fear of a possible clash between the West and the Soviet Union had me trembling now and again as I sat mindlessly weaving.

Particularly alarming were reports of confrontations, often bordering on hostility, between American and Soviet forces. Accounts of looting mounted, alleging that the Red Army had been hauling out trainloads of industrial equipment and household assets.

Could these developments signal another war?

I feared the European continent would sink further into bloodshed, of possible gargantuan proportions, impeding our ability to travel. *Will we ever be able to leave Uzbekistan and go home to Dubno? And where will we wander next with our parents – if they are indeed still alive?*

***

The Soviet Union had suffered by far the heaviest losses, bearing the brunt of the war. Yet it emerged as the war's primary victor. In the process, it overran and dominated huge swaths of liberated countries. Truman, concerned by the prospect of losing Europe to the Soviet Union, sought cautiously to isolate his erstwhile partner. It prompted the United States to turn its former enemy, Germany, into the main bulwark against the Red Menace.

As US forces, of both lower and higher levels, embarked on a mission to befriend the Germans, who, despite defeat, continued their hostility toward Jews, I worried the US would turn her back on us.

With great relief, I read about an upcoming summit to take place at Potsdam, in Berlin's Soviet zone. Radio Moscow soon filled the airwaves with the exciting news that US President Harry Truman, British Prime

Minister Winston Churchill, and Marshall Joseph Stalin would all attend and decide how the Allies should govern Germany, resolve peace-treaty issues and re-establish order in Europe.

Rabbi Zuckerman informed me daily of the conference's proceedings, which I supplemented by reading press releases available at the institute.

The conference came to a temporary halt on 26 July, during which time British election results revealed Churchill's stunning defeat, with Clement Attlee, of the opposition Labour Party, stepping up as new prime minister of Great Britain. The conference resumed on 28 July with Attlee representing the British government.

Meanwhile, rumour had it that the United States had developed a new weapon of immense power. News leaked from the conference revealed that the weapon in question was an atomic bomb, which the US had successfully tested.

Just days after the conference concluded, on 6 August news that the United States had dropped an atomic bomb on Hiroshima stunned the world. A week later, another bomb was dropped on Nagasaki. The immense blasts, which caused the immediate deaths of hundreds of thousands, with many more victims maimed and poisoned by radiation, brought Japan to her knees. Overnight, America became the dominant power on the world stage, with President Truman leading the charge.

9

The Liberation of the Camps

I became aware of the death camps in the German-occupied territories of the Soviet Union as far back as early August 1944, when I came across Ilya Ehrenburg's accounts in *Izvestia*, an official government newspaper. Ehrenburg, one of the Soviet Union's most prominent war correspondents and a recipient of the Order of Lenin, visited the Maly Trostenets death camp near Minsk, Belarus.

The Germans built the camp shortly after overrunning the Belarus territories in the fall of 1941, to 'concentrate' Jews from Minsk and other nearby cities. The inmates were subsequently transported to the nearby woods where they were shot en masse. The well-choreographed *danse macabre* of using the camp as a staging area for assembling victims on their way to death enabled the murderers to open these hell-gates for a flood of other victims from Poland and elsewhere in Europe. By late spring 1944, when German troops retreated, Trostenets had witnessed the murders of approximately 550,000 victims, ranking among the earliest German-built and German-run death camps in Eastern Europe.

The Soviet press continued to report on several concentration and death camps liberated by the advancing Red Army. Their liberation of the Majdanek-Lublin concentration camp, well-publicized in the Soviet press, exposed the atrocities carried out by the Germans.

As Eisenhower's Expeditionary Force continued its advance from the west toward Germany, it came face-to-face with the hellish camps. Sporadic articles in the Soviet press revealed liberation scenes of ghoulish walking skeletons, stacks of bleeding bodies, some still in the final throes of death, and crematoria still spewing the ash of human remains. The horrors exceeded any that the Allied military, including its superiors, had witnessed prior.

These shocking revelations, which came to occupy conversations among Samarkand's refugees, overwhelmed me, emotionally and mentally. *How could such barbarism take place? How could the people of Beethoven, Schiller and Goethe commit such unspeakable crimes?*

10

Goodbye, Samarkand

In mid-August Luba told me that Osher Balaban had indeed secured for us a permit to leave. She glowed with excitement as she delivered the good news, and I, of course, shared her happiness. *Maybe she's right – that we'll go home and reunite with our parents.* But as the days went on my thoughts darkened. *Hasn't Luba written dozens of letters home and received no reply?*

Time and again, I had read in *Pravda*, *Izvestia* and the army newspaper *Red Star*, that the Red Army had uncovered numerous mass graves on the outskirts of abandoned towns in the part of Poland where we had lived. I had a premonition that my parents, along with the rest of our family, had perished and were buried in those mass graves. I didn't want to dash Luba's hopeful expectations, but I feared the worst.

Later that month, Luba announced that she had found a man willing to buy our looms and our small business.

'What about the Zuckermans?' I asked.

'They decided to stay here awhile longer with their cousin.'

'Then what about Moniek?'

Luba grinned. 'Moniek will come with us.'

Her joyfulness pained me. And I didn't dare tell her about Mahdu, lest she make fun of – or disown – me. Indecision tore at me. I had found somebody I cared for, who had, in turn, expressed love for me. *Should I abandon Mahdu, or the thought of returning home?*

∗∗∗

During the first week of September I went to the institute to pick up my graduation documents, and to see Mahdu, who had recently returned from visiting her parents.

Her face lit up when we met, and she retrieved from a small bag a pair of woolen gloves that Sarrat had knitted for me, along with a silk scarf from her mother, Rashmi, while conveying to me their loving greetings. 'The people on the farms were glad to hear that you're all right. They're fond of you and miss you a lot, Meesha.' She had just begun her nursing studies at

Cover and inside page of my degree from the Uzbek Economic Institute, from 1945.

the institute, and she spoke with enthusiasm about the subjects she would be studying and her wonderful teachers. She also told me that she had her own room in a dormitory. 'Do you want to come up and see?'

My heart pounded as we climbed the two storeys to her little room, equipped with basic student furnishings.

She invited me to sit on the couch, which also served as a bed, and pulled a low table in front of it. 'Let me prepare you a modest bite to eat.' She came back with some flatbread and delicious olive spread. 'Now tell me, Meesha,' she said, taking a seat beside me, 'how did you spend the summer?'

I shared that we had purchased a second loom and that we were making quite a bit of money. 'Money makes one powerful,' I said with a chuckle. 'And that's how I'm beginning to feel.'

'So what are you going to do with all that money, big shot?' She slid closer. 'And what about the institute?'

I told her that I had come to pick up my graduation papers.

'So you're an economist now?' She was startled that I had finished my courses in such a short time. 'What do you want to do next?'

I summoned all my courage and blurted out that my sister had obtained papers for us to travel back home, where we had lived before the war.

Her face darkened. 'I thought I heard you say your parents and all your relatives were killed?'

'Maybe they have been,' I conceded. 'But it's possible they've survived and are anxiously awaiting my sister's and my return.'

We fell silent for a time before Mahdu spoke again, insisting that I not make any rash decisions and adding that she felt confident her father and uncle would be most eager to take advantage of my degree and abilities.

She squeezed my hand and gazed at me, her eyes filling with tears. 'Do you remember my telling you a couple of years ago that I liked you? I was seventeen then, brave, but wrong. In truth, I love you. I love you very much, in fact.' She pressed my fingers to her warm lips and kissed them.

'I love you too.' I embraced and kissed her. Suddenly, my whole torso throbbed with desire, and I ejaculated. Flustered, I let go.

'Don't be ashamed,' she said. 'It's nothing to be embarrassed about. I have lived all my life on a farm, remember?' She offered a sly smile. 'But next time, don't waste that precious treasure.'

She led me to the small bathroom, where I cleaned up. When I returned to the room, I sat next to her on the couch.

'But look, you're all wet now!' she exclaimed with a giggle. 'So you must stay until it dries.' Her expression grew serious. 'I don't want you to go – do you hear me? Please, don't leave. I'll make you happy, Meesha. We'll have a beautiful life here.'

The depth of her feelings, her determination, shook me to the core. *Maybe she's right*, I thought. I pictured myself living with Mahdu, among Uzbeks. *But I am not an Uzbek.* Then another thought occurred to me: *Nor am I Jewish!*

During four years of exile, Luba and I had never celebrated the Sabbath or any other Jewish holiday. The torrent of conflicts began to tear me apart. I felt myself floating in mid-air, without mooring.

'Meesha, Meesha.' Mahdu woke me from my reverie. 'Come back to me. I love you.'

I grasped her hand. 'Mahdu, I must go back to see whether my parents are still alive or hiding somewhere. I feel guilty that I abandoned them.'

'So you'd rather abandon me!' She burst out crying and fell into my arms.

After a few moments, I composed myself and released her, speaking softly but firmly. 'I'm sorry. I must go. Please forgive me for disappointing you.'

'Goodbye, Meesha,' she sobbed.

I stood and turned and walked out the door. My heart felt heavy as I hurried down the stairs and continued on to the institute. *Will I ever see Mahdu again?*

Memories of previous partings sifted through my mind – from parents, family and friends. My goodbye to Sophie, my high school sweetheart in Dubno, on the day I left, still pierced my heart. Now, along with Mahdu, it seemed Luba, too, would soon disappear from my life.

I felt as if I was in a big, empty chamber with no markers of human life or contact.

I was alone.

***

In mid-September 1945, Moniek, Luba and I boarded a train to Krasnovodsk in Turkmenistan, on the eastern shore of the Caspian Sea. We embarked as legitimate passengers, rather than jumping on the train like hobos, as we had so many times in the past. I felt more secure using a travel permit, despite it being purchased illegally through Osher Balaban's offices. Yosef and his wife, Lena, had stayed behind to finalize their departure with the authorities of the collective farm.

We entered the wagon, each of us carrying a single valise, though ones much larger than those Luba and I had left home with four years earlier. They contained warm clothing for the coming winter, along with samples of cloth I had woven, the designs of which made me proud. We deposited our luggage on racks above three empty seats on adjoining benches. I sat with two other passengers to my left, while Moniek and Luba sat as a couple on the other bench.

As the train pulled out of Samarkand Station, the conductor came by and carefully reviewed our documents. 'You have a long way to travel,' he said. 'Be careful with your belongings.' He added, 'I'll look out for your luggage. Where is it?'

Luba pointed, then took out twenty roubles, folded them, and shook the man's hand. 'Thank you very much, *Tovarisch* (comrade).'

'I'm pretty sure he's an NKVD agent,' she whispered after he left. 'I hope I gave him enough to keep him off our backs.'

I didn't ask Luba how she knew this, but she'd had plenty of experience dealing with the NKVD in the market where she bartered cloth for daily necessities.

I leaned back and fell deeply into my thoughts. Over the past few months loneliness had become my constant companion. I had by now resigned myself to losing Luba – her care and love for me. She and Moniek were understandably in love and excited to go home and start a life together. Meanwhile, doubts clouded my mind. *Should I abandon this country, bad as it is, in search of the unknown?*

Mahdu's sweetness had overwhelmed me – had awakened me as a man for the first time since Sophie, whom I had urged to leave home with Luba and me. Sophie had refused, and I had serious doubts whether she was still alive. Mahdu, by contrast, was very much alive and ever so lovely. *Maybe I should have stayed.*

Ever since fleeing, Luba and I had longed to return home to our parents, but Luba's queries had come back unanswered. Hadn't I heard enough, read enough, to determine that my hometown, like the others the Germans had occupied, lay in ruins, free of Jews? I felt like Shakespeare's Hamlet, who said, 'Better to bear those ills we have than fly to others that we know not of.'

The Soviet regime treated ordinary citizens harshly, depriving them of means for a decent living, but it treated engineers and scientists exceptionally well. Those were the fields I planned to pursue. My excellent grades at the institute, including those received in economics, physics, and chemistry, bolstered my confidence that I would be successful.

And I liked the people in Samarkand – Russian and Uzbek alike. They treated me well, never looking down on me because I was a Jew. They seemed to me more approachable and softer than the Polish Catholics, and they often unveiled to me a richer soul and a greater sensitivity than the Europeans I had known before the war. They sang a lot, in the streets, in classrooms, at work, or during study. I felt a cultural kinship with many of my classmates.

I had come here as a teen, ignorant of the ways of the world, during a vicious war. It was here that I matured. It was here that I finished high school and went beyond, to get a university degree. And it was here that I learned the resilience and might of the nation. I had often heard people refer to their country as 'Mother Russia.' I, too, felt the country shielding me, as a mother would, from the jungle-like tumult of the war.

I continued my reverie as the train wheels clicked and clacked over the spaces between the iron rails.

Then, as if awakened from a dream, I whispered, 'Are you stupid, thinking like that?' An image of a salmon swimming with all its might upstream to return to – and spawn – where it had come from came to my mind, prompting an overwhelming desire to go home. *I must go on, never give up. There might be no one else in the family on my mother's or father's side to carry on.* My mission now was to return and find out what had happened and, if need be, rescue what I could.

Having set my thoughts forward rather than back, I closed my eyes and dozed off.

The screeching brakes of the train woke me. Out the window, I saw that we were approaching a rural station. I straightened and yawned. I noted the empty left-most seat in my row where a young man in his twenties had been sitting. Instinctively, I looked up and saw that my valise was missing.

'Moniek!' I shouted. 'Come help me.'

We ran toward the car's exit and spotted the man waiting for the doors to open.

I hit him with all my force. 'That's my valise, you thief.' I thought of my father's lost watch.

'Sorry,' the young man said, letting go of my meagre belongings.

The commotion brought the conductor to the scene, but the exit door opened just as he approached, and the thief leapt down onto the platform and hurried away.

The conductor gave a shrug, and Moniek and I returned to our seats.

***

Two long days later, we arrived in Krasnovodsk. A day after that, we secured passage to cross the Caspian Sea and landed on the western shore of Baku, Azerbaijan.

From there, we travelled by train to Odessa, Ukraine, a port on the Black Sea. Odessa gave me my first shock of the death of a Jewish city. Prior to the war, nearly half the city's inhabitants had been Jewish. They prospered and gave rise to Jewish scholarship, writers of the Enlightenment, talented poets, as well as successful businessmen and manufacturers. It was the home of Bialik and Tchernichovsky, foremost Jewish poets; it had given birth to Sholem Aleichem, the popular Jewish writer. Odessan Jews had led the city's culture and music as well as its rich social fabric. From all my readings, Odessa was a beautiful city before the war, a bustling metropolis. But there was no sign of a Jew when we landed. And my questions to strangers of where they had all gone, were answered with a smirk: 'They died during the war.'

Our stop in Kiev a few days later confirmed the horrifying reality. Most of Kiev's Jews had been shot and buried in a ravine called Babi Yar.

11

Joy and Sorrow in Lvov

A week after leaving Samarkand, we arrived in Lvov, the largest city of south-eastern Poland. Roughly half of its several hundred thousand inhabitants had been Jewish before the German invasion. We found a synagogue open to refugees and secured a small corner in one of the rooms, with two benches to sleep on. Moniek and I shared one of the wider benches.

In the middle of the night, Luba tugged on my shirt. 'Mekhel, please go and sleep on my bench,' she whispered with a tremor in her voice. 'I'd be most thankful if you would.'

I obliged.

The next morning, Moniek explained that he and Luba had decided to get married, and he wanted to find a rabbi without delay. Later that day, I witnessed the wedding of Moniek and Luba. Although overcome with emotion while looking into the eyes of the newly-weds, I felt much more secure and hopeful.

Another witness, a thin man in his thirties with dark hair and dark eyes, had approached Luba before the ceremony, introducing himself as Yakov Hirsch from Dubno, our hometown. 'I knew your parents in the ghetto,' he'd said. 'I'll speak to you later. Mazel tov! Mazel tov!'

After the ceremony, the rabbi led us to a small room for refreshments.

I was troubled to see Luba crying in Moniek's arms.

'What's the matter?' I asked.

'Where's Mom?' she said. 'Where's Dad? They should be here.' She managed a weak smile. 'I'll be all right, Mekhel. Don't worry.'

Half an hour later, as we lingered, Yakov came back, accompanied by an attractive, well-dressed woman with red hair and a wealth of freckles. 'I'm Sarah Gochberg,' she said, turning to Luba. 'Do you remember me? We were classmates.'

'Of course, yes, Sarah. I remember you well.' She and Luba embraced.

We picked up our few belongings and left the synagogue with Sarah and Yakov leading the way. A few minutes later, we were climbing the stairs of a large brick building. When we reached the top of the second flight,

Sarah stepped to a door and opened it wide, inviting us to tour her spacious dwelling.

'This is beautiful,' Luba said. 'How did you come by such a gorgeous apartment?'

Sarah flashed a broad smile. 'I married a wonderful man.' She went on to explain that her husband, Sasha, was a colonel in the Soviet army who had connections. A successful businessman, he treated her like a queen.

'I hope you can stay here with us for a while,' she said. She then invited us into the kitchen, where she prepared some tea and began telling us of her ordeal during the war.

On the fifth or sixth day after their arrival in Dubno, the Germans had gathered the town's most prominent Jews – two rabbis, several well-to-do businessmen, and roughly a hundred other professionals – and hanged them in the middle of the market square. A few weeks later, they ordered all Jews to wear white armbands bearing the blue Star of David. Soon after, they began apprehending Jewish women at random and hauled them away, never to be heard from again. In October 1941, on Simchat Torah (an upbeat holiday honouring the Torah), they organized the first 'action' by picking up hundreds of young people and taking them to the Jewish cemetery, where they were shot and buried in deep ditches.

Toward the end of 1941, the Germans constructed a ghetto in the town, enclosing four streets, including Berka Yoselevicza and Stara, where they starved Jews by reducing rations of bread and eliminating all other food. At the same time, inhabitants were ordered to perform hard labour for long hours. Sarah worked as a seamstress from dawn till evening. The winter months were particularly brutal, bringing cold, famine, and rampant illness that took many of the lives of the very old and the very young. This was followed by mass executions to liquidate the ghetto.

In April 1942, during Passover, the Germans, with the help of Ukrainian gendarmes, cordoned off at night a third or so of the ghetto and forced the Jews from the segregated area into the streets, where they were hauled – on trucks and on foot – to the outskirts of town, near the river. There they forced the men to dig large ditches – for anti-aircraft defence, they said. When the ditches were complete, they lined up row upon row of Jews, machine-gunned them, and bulldozed the dead into the massive channels, covering them with the dug-out earth.

A few managed to escape and return to the ghetto to warn of the atrocities. That was when Sarah's mother and father ordered her to leave.

'I'll tell you more later about my miraculous survival,' Sarah said, setting a plate of pastries on the table. 'Let us first have something to eat.'

Sarah's deeply troubling account left me stunned. I had, of course, read of the appalling crimes of the Germans, and I feared the worst. But this personal account from a survivor pained me with an intensity I had never before experienced, awakening me to the dark and likely reality that Mom and Dad and all my relatives were dead.

Later, during dinner, Yakov told us that when the Germans set up the ghetto, our home became the housing for twenty or so people, he and his parents among them. Also residing there were our grandmother; our aunt with her little boy; our uncle, his wife, and their two daughters; and several of Dad's relatives.

One day, after the first wave of executions in April 1942, our parents left the ghetto to find our father's friend, a Ukrainian who lived in a village near Dubno. Toward evening, they returned, with Mom near collapse. A young SS man named Hoffman had recognized Mom and turned our parents back, whipping them along the way. According to Mom, Hoffman, a classmate of Luba's, had, on several occasions, been a visitor in our home.

'I remember him,' Luba said, her eyes troubled. 'When and why did he join the SS?'

'That I can't tell you,' Yakov replied. 'But many Poles, particularly Ukrainians, co-operated with the Germans.' He shrugged. 'Hoffman is a German name. Maybe his parents or grandparents were German or Austrian. Who knows?'

This incident convinced our parents to stay on in their home.

Three months later, the Germans initiated another action, this time getting rid of all older people and young children – any and all Jews who were unable to work. They swept through the remaining part of the ghetto and hauled away about three thousand people, among them our grandmother, aunt, nephew and several of my father's elderly relatives, leaving our parents, our uncle Avrum and his wife, and Yakov and his parents in the home. Dad wanted to run, stating that he longed to see his children again, but Mom refused to leave for fear of what might happen to them should they be caught.

Shortly after the second wave of killings, Dad set upon building an underground bunker, explaining that it would span from the cellar to the end of the property, and possess an opening in the adjoining lumberyard. The group started digging, mostly in the evenings after returning from work. Every day another foot or two. It was back-breaking work, but they managed to complete a fair bit of the structure, well-hidden in the cellar.

In late September, when it became apparent that the Germans were planning to exterminate the remaining Jews, Yakov's parents, along with our father, urged him to flee. In October 1942, on Simchat Torah, the Germans killed the remaining five thousand Jews, liquidating the Dubno ghetto.

Yakov made his way to the woods, some ten miles from Dubno, and spent the remaining year and a half with a group of other young Jewish men and women in the forest, rummaging for food in the fields at night. Winter brought death to several of the group. Nevertheless, a dozen of them managed to survive until the Russians arrived in February 1944.

We listened in silence, though Luba wept quietly. A throbbing pain pulsed through me as I pictured my parents, emaciated and weak, embracing each other as they awaited execution. In my mind, they appeared frozen, yet at peace. They stood vividly before me, so close I thought I could touch them. Remorse filled my gut, for not being with them when they needed me most.

We rose from the table, and I gently embraced a shivering, whimpering Luba before we parted for the night.

***

The next day, we learned the unbelievable story of Sarah's survival.

After the first wave of executions in the spring of 1942, Sarah's parents made arrangements with a Czech family to find shelter for her. One evening, Sarah took a small bundle of belongings and all the money and jewellery her parents had and left the ghetto. The Czech, a business associate of her father's, met her at an appointed place and accompanied her to the home of an elderly couple, who made arrangements for her to stay in their attic, which had a small entry reachable only by ladder.

The couple delivered to Sarah morning and evening meals, and emptied her chamber pot. She had to be absolutely quiet, and when she cried, which she did a lot, she was to pack her mouth with a towel. Hardest of all was keeping her sanity amid constant loneliness and sorrow. She lost track of the passing time.

Finally, in the spring of 1944, she heard commotion and shouting. 'The Russians are here!'

Released from her prison, Sarah feared for her life, finding no Jews in Dubno and her home having been taken over by Ukrainians. Slowly amid peril, she made her way to Lvov, where she met Sasha.

How was so much insanity allowed to unfold? I wondered. *Where did such hatred, such beastliness, come from?* The air and soil around us in this place seemed as though drenched with poison, and I concluded that we could not stay.

During our two weeks with Sarah, we witnessed the beginnings of a revival of Jewish life in Lvov. Jewish refugees from Soviet Central Asia arrived daily. NGOs (non-governmental organizations), such as the American Jewish Joint Distribution Committee – the Joint, for short – helped new arrivals find temporary shelter and a means of subsistence.

Jewish communal life began to bud, with new arrivals reopening abandoned synagogues, schools for the young, and creating homes for the sick and the elderly. A new resolve to recoup their homes and means of making a living reanimated the resilient survivors, sparking an unquenchable longing to emigrate to Palestine and build a Jewish homeland. Their stay in Lvov would be temporary and not without fear.

12

The Refugees, the Survivors and the DP Camps

The first wave of dislocation began shortly after the Germans marched into Poland in September 1939. Approximately two hundred thousand Polish Jews fled the western half of Poland following the German blitzkrieg. They headed to the eastern half of Poland, soon to be occupied by the Soviet Union. In the following two years, the NKVD deported nearly all these refugees to Siberia. Subsequently, these desperate innocents found their way to the Soviet republics of Central Asia, thanks to an agreement between Stalin and the Polish government-in-exile. Among them were my brother-in-law Moniek Perlman, and his brother Yosef.

My late wife, Regina Chanowicz, and her family endured the similar good fortune of being saved in Kyrgyzstan after being forced to leave their hometown of Suwalki in the western half of Poland.

Another contingent of approximately fifty thousand Polish Jews in eastern Poland – occupied by the Soviet Union in1939 – miraculously fled the rapidly advancing German army in June 1941 and ended up in Uzbekistan or other Soviet Central Asian republics, among them my sister and I. After the war's end, approximately two hundred fifty thousand Polish Jews, having lived through the horrors of the war and Stalin's regime of terror, reversed their flight across the Soviet Union and found their way to displaced persons (DP) camps in West Germany. They were joined by a stream of Jewish refugees fleeing territories newly occupied by, or just ahead of, the Red Army. Their influx would continue unabated well into the early 1950s, swelling the DP population to several hundred thousand.

***

Lvov became an important hub for refugees from the East, as well as for survivors from nearby concentration and death camps. During our weeks-long stay in Lvov, I met a few concentration and death camp survivors, several new arrivals from the East, and a few Joint aid workers as well. Their accounts, along with those of the information services, including the Yiddish-American press that often reached Lvov, provided me an alarming picture of the state of survivors, particularly those who were Jewish, in the months following liberation.

From survivors of the Belzec concentration camp, I learned that liberation of the camps brought waves of exultation, bordering on delirium, for inmates still able to comprehend what was happening. The majority of survivors, however, were too far gone, physically and mentally, to appreciate their change in status. Continued deplorable living conditions in the camps, along with heart-breaking news of lost family members and friends, further dashed their hopes for resuming normal lives.

I heard accounts from Joint aid workers that most survivors continued to live in similar hellish conditions as before, with cruel guards – some former members of the SS – near-starvation food rations, and crowded, filthy sleeping facilities. Old animosities between the various ethnic and national groups contributed to a hostile and threatening environment for Jewish inmates. The lack of medical care exacted a heavy toll on the weakest inmates by way of malnutrition, as well as unsupervised overeating of food sent by NGOs and charitable organizations.

In time, I learned that the United States Army bore the heaviest burden of rescuing and rehabilitating survivors. Trained to fight, the army found itself ill-prepared to deal with the atrocities it witnessed. Its immediate mission then became to provide barely adequate shelter and food to survivors.

The army's other primary objective was to resettle as many inmates as it could. A significant number of survivors, however, could not, or would not, return to their countries of origin, now occupied by the Red Army, for fear of retribution. Jewish survivors, uniquely, soon found there were no relatives and no homes to return to. Further, they feared that returning to their homes would provoke Jewish killings of the kind that had taken place in Kielce in July of 1945.

The living conditions for Jewish inmates were little better than before their liberation, albeit minus the gas chambers.

✶✶✶

The Yiddish-American press reported that shortly after the liberation of the camps, a barrage of reports about the alarming condition of Jewish survivors began to reach the US press and members of Congress. The news catapulted to President Truman's desk. In one article, I read of Truman appointing a special envoy – Earl Harrison, vice president of the University of Pennsylvania and dean of its law school – to inspect and report on the DP camps in the US zone, as well as those in the other Allied zones of Germany. Another item referred to Harrison's scathing report on the condition of DP inmates in the United States Occupation Zone. Harrison's recommendation, to segregate Jewish inmates into their own camps, proved to be most beneficial.

Later, I learned that Truman had sent a critical letter to Eisenhower, reprimanding the general for the sorry state of Jewish survivors and commanding him, in harsh terms, to improve their situation.

These developments began to take hold of the US Army's camp administration, but not without significant bumps in the road. For one, General Eisenhower struggled to implement Truman's orders due to resistance from senior army leaders, including General George S. Patton, commander of the Third Army, who was an avowed anti-Semite.

Notwithstanding these difficulties, the US Army announced a policy of granting sanctuary to the homeless roaming the US Occupation Zone. This opened the door for thousands of refugees fleeing the East ahead of the Red Army and swelled the camp population in Bavaria, the southern zone of US occupation.

News spread by word of mouth that Landsberg, near Munich, had become a Jewish refugee camp. That caught my attention, and I viewed it as a hopeful haven, a rescue island in the middle of a stormy sea.

13

Coming Home: Bearing Witness

'Beware of the Ukrainians,' people in Lvov warned us. 'They were more brutal than the Germans, and they still are. They have stolen Jewish property, and they fear that returning Jews will try to take it back.' They also warned that Jewish life in smaller towns had been extinguished, and, further, that travel outside of Lvov posed great danger as Ukrainian partisans fighting the Soviets roamed the roads, eager as ever to kill more Jews.

In October 1945, Luba, Moniek and I began our trek home, despite warnings of the dangerous traveling conditions. We had planned to go by train but found it impossible to obtain permits, so we waited at the main road going north from Lvov, where we managed to wave down a truck driver who agreed to drop us in Dubno on his way north to Rovno. Naturally, his willingness to accommodate was motivated by the money we offered.

A chilly gray afternoon greeted us as we arrived in Dubno, where we walked with muted hope to our home, a kilometre or so away from the main road. We quickened our pace along the empty cobblestone streets in anticipation of seeing our house. Memories of a happy childhood crowded my mind. *Will I find any traces of it inside?*

My heart sank as we drew close. The house at 256 Berka Yoselevicza was now worn and shabby, with a broken fence, peeling pink paint, and its brick entrance obscured by a mass of overgrown weeds.

'Let me try to enter,' Luba said.

Moniek and I stayed behind as she climbed the few steps and knocked.

The door cracked open. 'What do you want?' a man asked in a Ukrainian accent.

'I was hoping to look at the house I used to live in,' Luba said quietly.

'Wait a minute.' He stepped away and returned a moment later, carrying a pitchfork nearly as tall as his diminutive form. 'Get out of here, you dirty Jews, or I'll kill you!'

After the man slammed the door in her face Luba, with tears in her eyes, came down and rejoined us. The idea that the Ukrainians who now occupied our home might have helped the Germans in their grisly task of killing my parents choked me with anger.

'We'd better find a place to stay before it gets dark,' Luba said. 'Perhaps we might try Uncle Avrum's place.'

Fearing another Ukrainian would chase us away, we knocked with trepidation on the door of our uncle's much larger home, a block away from our own.

A short, stocky woman greeted us warmly as we introduced ourselves. 'My name is Rivka Chayat,' she said, inviting us inside. 'I'm a sister of Gitl Guberman, Avrum's wife.' She took our wet coats and invited us to sit and warm ourselves in the living room, where we met her husband, Jacob. She returned with tea and pastries.

We told Rivka and Jacob briefly about our four years deep inside the Soviet Union. She told us about her miraculous survival with a peasant family, her return to Dubno to reclaim her sister's home, and about meeting and marrying Jacob.

'Unfortunately,' she said, 'there are hardly any Jews left in Dubno. The Germans killed them all, including my sister and her family. Your parents and relatives, too.' With a sigh, she looked toward her husband. 'I'm not sure whether we should stay either.'

Rivka prepared dinner for us and then showed us around the house, inviting us to stay in one of the bedrooms. Before retiring for the evening, she suggested we try to obtain from the town administrator the proper documents of ownership to our house, and that of our grandmother.

After Luba resolved to visit the town hall the next day, I made up my mind to look around the ruins of my hometown. I was up early the following morning, after a fitful night, and left on my solitary tour.

As I walked the ominously quiet street, I remembered how it had once been filled in the early-morning hours – children on their way to school, people rushing to work. It appeared unreal, like a painting instead of an actual neighbourhood. Anger rose inside me as I made my way west toward my old house, where, a day earlier, the Ukrainian usurper had threatened Luba and slammed our own front door in her face.

Once again, memories flooded my mind as I stood in front of the shabby structure that had once been my home. The acacia tree still stood in the front yard, with its little wraparound bench, where Luba used to sit and read for hours. The barely visible remains of the vegetable garden brought recollections of Dad and me tilling the small plot and planting cucumbers, tomatoes, lettuce, cabbage, scallions, squash, and sunflowers. I remembered the joy of seeing the plants grow and the vegetables ripen. I remembered how, foolishly, I had climbed up on the roof of the garage on the second day of the war between the Germans and the Soviet Union, to watch the German planes pass overhead. They could have strafed me, I realized now, being four years older and wiser.

I turned back and headed past my uncle's house to Panienska, the town's main street. On it was my grandmother's house, which dated back to the early 1800s, having been built by my great-grandparents. They had supplied provisions to General Suvorov's army during the Napoleonic Wars, thereby earning the Suvorkhi nickname, which passed on to subsequent generations and which made me proud. I used to spend hours perusing the files of my grandfather's commercial transactions, and possibly of the earlier generations of the Gubermans, dealing with hops, flour, and grain, in addition to meat. Grandmother's tales of her years of suffering and her struggles to feed her two sons and four younger daughters, with Peshia, her youngest, barely out of infancy, came to my mind.

I knocked on the door of the portion of the spacious house in which my grandmother had lived. A middle-aged woman greeted me with suspicion.

After I explained my relationship to the house's owner, she invited me in. I recognized the layout and furnishings and expressed my surprise that it looked the same as it had before the war. She told me that German officers had occupied the house, and that she and her husband, a Soviet official, had been living in the apartment for more than a year. Another Soviet official occupied the other part of the house.

I excused myself after sharing a brief account of my war experiences and walked west on Panienska Street, heading toward the house where Sophie, my gymnasium sweetheart, had lived. As I opened the latch on the gate and stepped into the backyard, I stopped, labouring to draw breath, and with a choking sensation in my throat. Sophie's voice rang out as clearly as on the day I had asked her, four years earlier, to run away with me and Luba: 'You talk like a true teenager,' she'd said. 'You make it sound like a picnic. Do you even have an address to go to?'

I crossed the porch and knocked on the door, but there was no answer. Peering through the window, I saw the same furniture that had been there on the day I parted with Sophie. I wondered what might have happened to her. Was she killed in one of the *Aktions*, or did she die from starvation or illness? What would Sophie have become had she lived? My pent-up rage at the fates of the Dubno Jews, who had been so viciously murdered, thundered to the surface, focused through my memories of this beautiful, talented and brilliant young woman.

I took the long way back to my uncle's house, past the famed castle, a magnificent structure located on an island of the Ikva River. Complete with moat and bridge, a red ceramic roof, and cannon posts guarding its long perimeter, the massive fort was the symbol of Dubno's military prowess of centuries past. I couldn't help but smile, recalling the number of times I had sat upon a schoolyard bench, painting its handsome façade.

I toyed with the idea of visiting the high school, but decided against it. My bitterness – for the Polish and Ukrainian classmates and teachers who had likely collaborated with the Germans to kill off my people – was palpable.

My sombre journey took me south toward the center of town, returning to Panienska, then Alexandrovna, the main commercial street. Approaching the farthest corner, I recognized the building, now boarded up, that my parents had used as their soft-goods store before the arrival of the Soviets in 1939. The once-thriving commercial centre of Dubno, that Jews had built and made prosperous, now stood abandoned.

I walked north, parallel to the Ikva, and came to the place where we had rented rowboats and had swum in the summertime. I passed the old *Tarbut* middle school, now in a state of total disrepair, where I'd learned Jewish history eight years earlier from a devoted Zionist who implored us to go to Palestine and build a Jewish home. His impassioned voice reverberated in my mind: 'There is no future for Jewish young people in Poland, or anywhere else, except in Palestine.'

I walked east on Berka Yoselevicza and knocked on the doors of my school friends' homes. When I received no response, I gave up and headed back to my uncle's house.

'If we're lucky,' Luba said, greeting me cheerfully, 'we might be able to sell our home.' She told me that the town hall's official registrar was able to verify our ownership of the house, and he promised to process appropriate papers in the next few days. 'I'm going to try to do the same for Grandmother's house.'

***

A few days after our arrival, Joseph Gitman, the son of one of two official rabbis in town, came to Dubno. He had studied in the late 1930s at the famous liberal rabbinic school in Warsaw called Tahkemoni and had returned home just before the war to be a teacher in the high school. A distant relative on my mother's side, he had taken a liking to Luba, and they had dated briefly, but Luba did not care for him in that way. After the

German invasion in June 1941, Joseph fled Dubno, ending his flight in Tashkent, the capital of Uzbekistan. After the war, he made his way back, taking a route similar to ours, and found a place to stay with a distant relative who had survived the war and eventually reclaimed his home.

I liked Joseph and felt a kinship with him. We began to take long walks around town. Our visit to the Great Synagogue, in particular, brought back sweet recollections. The imposing structure, visible for miles around, had been built a hundred years earlier at the height of Jewish prosperity in Dubno.

'What's happened here?' I asked the sentry in front of the synagogue's closed door.

'It was turned into a stable for the Gestapo horses,' the man replied. 'Now the town is trying to clean it out to make some use of it.'

I had once sung as a soloist in the choir of the famed chazzan (cantor) Zalman Sherman: 'Haben Yakir Li Efrayim' ('I will remember my dear son, Ephrayim…'). Cantor Sherman set me standing on a chair so that the High Holiday worshippers crowding the large hall would be able to see me. The memory transported me to a world beautiful and far removed from the brutal reality that followed. *How could such a profound transformation occur in a few short years?*

Cantor Sherman's passionate plea on Yom Kippur – 'Do not abandon us; do not remove your holy spirit from us' – jolted me with pain. God did abandon my family, my people. I shared my thoughts with Joseph.

'Being bitter will not help us now, Mekhel,' Joseph said. 'We have to go on. We have to fight for a better world, despite the catastrophe.'

'I feel our prayers to an Almighty God have been in vain,' I replied as we made our way back to my uncle's house. 'And our belief in a God who turned out to be blind to this tragedy has been a farce.'

'Mekhel, Mekhel.' Joseph patted my back. 'You certainly said a mouthful, but it is not quite correct. You're taking the words of the prayers too literally. God is certainly not a king, not a general. He doesn't have any mechanized armies to fight evil men like Hitler. God is an idea, a concept, not a corporeal being. And the prayers are texts, written by talented poets and dreamers to represent the idea of God as they understood it, and in a way that it will relate to people's conception of God.'

His words startled me. 'What do you mean by an idea, a concept?' My tone was strident, challenging.

'God as an idea is the embodiment of perfection – perfection of justice, fairness, compassion, goodness and peace. It's the ultimate standard of human behaviour, in resonance with the harmony of the universe.'

'And what do you do with this idea?'

'You strive for it. You try to make others strive for it. You convince people – all people – to achieve those ultimate standards. And then, and only then, will you be able to avoid the likes of Hitler.'

'And meanwhile, how would you prevent violence and crime?'

'We Jews talk about the Messianic era. We have no date for it, and the belief that the Messiah will arrive on a white horse one day is also a legend. I rather think that each day we do some good, each day we live in peace, we advance the coming of the Messiah. We advance the concept of God.'

I bade goodbye to Joseph, who left to try to reclaim his property. His words lingered in my mind as I walked back to my uncle's house, compelling me to think beyond the struggles of a life that had overwhelmed me for so long. I admired his poetic words, and his erudition humbled me. He knew well the Hebrew texts, had thought much about religion and God, and spoke with such ease. But his pronouncements failed to quiet my inner turmoil. How could I, after all, ever reconcile my parents' desperate cries to God to be rescued as they were being led to the killing fields?

The next day, Joseph came to Uncle's house, and Rivka introduced us to survivors of the ghetto and executions. One of them, Reuben Cantor, offered to accompany us to the mass grave of the last action, where some five thousand Jews, including Reuben's parents, Joseph's parents, and my parents and relatives – the remainder of the ghetto – were murdered on 5 October 1942.

The early-autumn day, though sunny in the morning, had turned drizzly by afternoon. As we walked, Reuben described the scene of the executions that he, although wounded, had miraculously managed to survive.

German soldiers and Ukrainian gendarmes and peasants lined up the Jews in groups of several dozen at the edge of a ditch that had been dug in the ravine next to the Ikva River. A young German, a chain-smoker of cigarettes, fired his machine gun at the victims, most of whom were still alive as bulldozers pushed them, one on top of the other, into the ditch.

That night, Reuben, who had been shot in the shoulder, freed himself from the dead and dying bodies, gathered up some clothes, and fled into the outlying forest. There he joined a group of fellow partisans who disrupted German supply lines by putting logs and other heavy objects on the tracks to derail trains and steal the goods and arms they carried.

Horrified, I asked, 'Why didn't the Jews fight back?'

'We had lost our will to live and all hope of surviving. Even if one could run away, running jeopardized the lives of everyone else in the ghetto. For example, if the number of people returning from work didn't match the number that had left the ghetto for work that morning, they would hang a dozen men as punishment. The ghetto was prison, ruled by vicious, armed beasts, and surrounded by vultures – Ukrainians – who took over Jewish property and homes and eagerly helped the Germans in their grisly tasks. Toward the end, we knew we would all die, and worse, we could do nothing about it.'

As we reached the ravine, I noticed a boy tending a few cows grazing in the lush field.

'Here,' Reuben said, 'look at all the scattered bones. This area, extending for several hundred metres, is filled with layers and layers of our martyrs. You see this corner here?' Reuben pointed. 'That's where I was able to get hold of some rocks and crawl out from the grave.'

The little-boy herder stopped by and stared at us.

'Whose bones are these?' I asked him.

'They are bones of wild animals,' he said and went off.

We stood, shocked into silence. How could one tolerate so easily the jarring clash – of bucolic quietude in the very place where only a few years before were heard the shrieks of men, women and children being led to their slaughter? I felt suddenly dizzy and cold. Unable to reconcile my being alive when so many had been exterminated – nearly the whole town – I pictured myself in the pit with my parents, grandmother, aunt, and little cousin, Heniek, barely five years old. I felt a bullet pierce my heart and warm blood spilling from my body. I imagined shovelfuls of heavy earth raining down on me, pressing me into the abyss. I was dying, and Mom and Dad were there with me. Nausea stirred my gut, and bile rose into my throat.

Joseph, Reuben and I said Kaddish (the prayer for the dead) and left.

On the way back to Uncle's house, I recalled the heart-rending prayer chanted by the famed cantor Jacob Koussevitzky in a concert he gave at the Great Synagogue before the war. 'Abeytmeeshomayimur'ay' ('Open your eyes, our God, and see...how we have been devastated...'). The prayer dated back to the twelfth century, when the crusaders slaughtered Jews throughout western Europe on their way to worship Christ in Jerusalem.

The plague of Jew hatred is alive and well, eight hundred years later.

I recounted our visit to Luba, telling her of the mass grave filled with skeletons, scattered skulls and limbs, and also relayed the tale of Reuben's miraculous escape. 'You must go and see it for yourself.'

But Luba was focused elsewhere. 'Mekhel, we must go on living,' she said. 'We cannot die with them. Remember, you're the only Kesler remaining in the world. We must go on.'

That night, I dreamed my parents lay next to me, and beyond them thousands of skeletons. I saw them as I had so many times before since witnessing the wounded, dying soldier on the train in Shepetovka – the train Luba and I had jumped onto after fleeing home four years earlier. Dad's throat had been slashed, with blood pouring from the wound. Mom lay to his right, her head set peacefully against his pale shoulder. Dad's eyes were open and looking straight at me.

I caressed his hair. '*Tatte*, Luba and I have come home, but there is no one here. They are all in mass graves. Are you and Mom there? You told me people were good. You taught me to have faith. But no one cared to stop the killings – not even God.'

After a long silence, Dad spoke. 'The earth has turned into *Tohu Vavohu* – waste and wilderness – and an evil darkness is sweeping over its abyss.'

'*Tatte*, I want to stay with you and Mom.'

'Go,' he whispered and closed his eyes.

'*Tatte*, I love you,' I cried.

But he did not answer.

I heard Mom whisper, 'I love you, Mekhel,' as I woke up, drenched with sweat.

Though overcome by the guilt of having lived through the slaughter, I accepted it as a necessary burden I would have to carry, even as I moved forward.

My visit to the mass grave convinced me that we could not stay in Dubno, and I readily agreed when Luba and Moniek suggested we leave quickly. Luba wasted no time finding a buyer for our house, and that of my grandmother. To my great surprise, a Russian businessman was interested in the properties, paying $250 for each, an unbelievable sum for us.

'Now we have enough to buy our way through the borders and into West Germany,' Luba exclaimed, showing me the crisp US fifty-dollar bills.

The next morning Luba, Moniek and I were on a train to Krakow, where we were set to join Moniek's mother and relatives.

***

Our route took us back through Lvov and thento Krakow, where we visited Moniek's mother, a priority upon arrival in the city, and were pleasantly surprised to find Yosef and Lena there as well. Moniek's mother, Eva Perlman, was a tall, stately woman with grey hair, a lined, angular face, broad lips and bright blue eyes. Despite the privations of the past years, she displayed much energy and vitality.

Her face lit up as she embraced Moniek, who stayed in his mother's arms a long while.

'What a miracle it is to see you all here!' she exclaimed. 'After so much tragedy, it's wonderful to see my boys well and married too. I can't believe my own eyes, but it's true, thank God. If only your father were here. Unfortunately, he did not survive, and tomorrow will be his yahrzeit (anniversary of his death). I have so much to tell you...' She exited the room, her voice choked with emotion. When she had composed herself, Eva returned, asking us to wash up before joining her in the kitchen, where she served soup filled with generous chunks of chicken. 'It's an unbelievable story,' she began, 'but miracles did happen, even during this dreadful period.' She told us of the deaths of the vast majority of the Jews in Krakow, and of her survival.

Shortly after entering Krakow in the fall of 1939, the Germans began to harass the Jews. They picked people at random and beat them or hanged them in public. They deprived Jews of food, seized Jewish property at will and made life unbearable. In the fall of 1940 they set up a ghetto and crowded all the Jews into a small area of the city. A few months later, they began the transfer of thousands of Jews to a nearby concentration camp at Plaszow.

Eva and several of her cousins had spent most of the war working in the factories of an industrialist named Oskar Schindler. 'I heard that Schindler saved 1,200 Jews!' she exclaimed, the blood rushing to her face.

A contractor who supplied strategic goods to the German army, Oskar Schindler had many connections with top German authorities in Krakow. When he decided to recruit Jewish people destined for the concentration camp to work in his factories, Moniek's cousin, Regina, who was hired on as a secretary, was among the first. She succeeded in convincing Schindler to select Moniek's mother, his uncles, and a few cousins to work for him, saving a good part of Moniek's family.

Unfortunately, the Germans had taken Moniek's father, along with some other men, out to work in a factory twenty or so miles from Krakow. From there, he was sent to another camp, where he became ill and died.

Eva's story made painfully clear the monstrous pattern of annihilation thrust upon Jewish communities throughout Eastern Europe. The Jews of Krakow had suffered the same dismal fate as the Jews of Lvov and Dubno.

***

Moniek's mother set up one of the bedrooms of her small apartment for the three of us to stay in. The next day, we met the cousin responsible for saving nearly half the Perlman family while working as a secretary for Mr. Schindler. An attractive woman in her early thirties – tall, slim, and vivacious, with large blue eyes and blonde hair – Regina Wolf exuded confidence and cheer.

'He was temperamental – often drunk,' she said of Oskar Schindler. 'An egotist, he nevertheless became obsessed with saving Jews otherwise destined for the gas chambers.'

Judenrein

© Copyright February 2008, Don Bloom, E. Brunswick, N.J.

Later in the day, another of Moniek's cousins, Naftali Eckstein, visited. He had spent several years in the Mauthausen concentration camp, where Moniek's father had died. Naftali, a stout man in his forties, with a round face and mischievous eyes, purveyed good humour and funny stories. A Jewish rescue group, Bricha, had engaged him to help Jews returning from the concentration camps, as well as from the Soviet Union, to migrate to West German DP camps.

∗∗∗

Soon after our arrival, Naftali arranged for us to leave Krakow through Czechoslovakia. Toward the end of December, Moniek's mother, Yosef, Lena, Moniek, Luba and I crossed the Polish-Czech border at Szchechin. From there we took a train to Prague, where we stayed for a few days. On Christmas Eve 1945, we found ourselves in a small border town across the River Saale from Hof, Germany.

Naftali's friends explained to us that Christmas Eve would be a good time to sneak across, since most of the guards would be off celebrating the holiday with their families. The friends had also arranged for guides to carry the women across the shallow river, while we men trailed behind in the rocky, knee-deep water. At one point, I lost my footing and fell in. Soaked through with ice-cold water, I shivered violently the rest of the way across.

Once on the German side, the guides led us to a small shack where we were to stay for the night. They covered me with blankets and slowly I began to warm up, further comforted by the realization that we were now safely in the US Occupation Zone of West Germany.

14

My Year in a DP Camp – Hope, Despair and Rebirth

My clothes were still wet when I awoke. Luba and Eva hovered over my shivering body, covering me with more blankets, with Luba assuring me that the owners of the hut were working to get me a change of clothes.

As soon as I was able to dress, we caught a train bound for Munich. Ironically, we felt freer and more secure in the murderers' den, the city that had incubated the Nazi scourge, than we had in our homeland.

We made our way to the office of the United Nations Relief and Rehabilitation Agency (UNRRA), where we were assigned to the displaced persons camp of Landsberg, the town famous for the jail where Hitler had written *Mein Kampf*, his manifesto on German control of the continent, which included his plan for exterminating the Jews.

Moniek, seeing my discomfort, embraced me. 'This is but a halfway house, nothing more.'

Before the war, the Landsberg camp had housed a military unit of the Wehrmacht. Later, it was converted to a Nazi concentration camp – a branch of the massive Dachau complex. By October 1944, there were more than five thousand prisoners in the camp, which was liberated by US forces in April 1945. It consisted of many barracks scattered over several acres and included recreational facilities. The camp itself stood apart from the main town where the German civilian population lived.

We were advised to stay within the compound.

The approximately five thousand residents of the camp at the time of our arrival were all Jewish survivors of the war, most of them having endured the tortures and horrors of the concentration camps. Some, like us, had fled to the Soviet Union. Homelessness was the primary registration requirement for residing in the camps, and we were certainly that. Homeless and stateless.

Luba, Moniek and I were assigned one large room in the barrack. Luba was able to locate a mobile partition and arranged for a smaller area in one corner of the room to be my 'new home,' as she called it. My furnishings amounted to a small cot and a nightstand with a lamp. Luba and Moniek had a large bed, a dining table, a small stand for a miniature electric stove and a sink with running water next to it. A toilet and two showers were down the hall and shared with occupants in other rooms. Moniek's mother, his older brother, Yosef, and his wife, Lena, were assigned another large room, a few rooms away from ours. Moniek's cousins were likewise accommodated in various parts of the same barrack.

UNRRA supplied us with blankets, sheets, pillows, towels, and daily rations of food. The food, at least initially, was a problem. Moniek, Luba and Moniek's brother, mother and cousins were strictly kosher, meaning that we were subsisting on the protein of canned tuna and eggs until kosher meat and chicken products arrived, courtesy of the Joint and the Agudath, in response to petitions signed by Orthodox Jews.

Soon, we were functioning as a family unit.

Luba took up teaching in the new camp school, while Moniek stayed busy working on a design for an electric razor he was inventing. Meanwhile, I enrolled in a course to study radio repair, to begin in February, offered by the Organization for Rehabilitation and Training (ORT). During the war, I had come to realize the importance of this means of communication.

In late January, I developed a high fever and was admitted into the camp infirmary. Even after the fever subsided, I remained weak and lethargic. The nightmares, of seeing and touching my bleeding, dying father, came back, and I pictured being with my whole family, crowded into our two-room home, sharing morsels of stale bread and spoonfuls of water. *Where did they get water?* I wondered. Surely the Germans had done away with water carriers.

I imagined holding Mom in my arms and wiping her tears, and then trying to cheer my sad father with songs I had sung at the Great Synagogue on the High Holidays. I was with them as the Gestapo chased them out of their home and into the streets, with wild dogs nipping at their heels and Ukrainians clubbing them and forcing them into columns before marching them to the outskirts of town. I stood beside them as they dug their own graves and later undressed for death. I clung to them as the bullets hit and the blood flowed as they fell into the grave and into the abyss.

The guilt and shame I felt at abandoning my parents was with me always, and my nightmares of deserting the Soviet army, which had diminished with time, had resurfaced, haunting me, making me feel like a traitor, small and feeble. Loneliness, too, gripped me. Luba had married, and I had no one left in the world who cared for me.

Beyond that, I feared the future. What hope was there for those of us remaining? What was the purpose of surviving in a jungle of beastliness and hostility?

My will to live began to crumble.

Then a young nurse appeared for night duty on our ward.

Stefa Aronowicz was slim and tall – a bit taller than I – with blond hair and blue eyes. Her soft smile and mellifluous voice lifted me out of my depression. She listened patiently as I shared my nightmares and doubts, and responded always with gentle authority, reminding me how lucky we were to be alive, how thankful we should be for surviving this unimaginable period of human history.

One evening, with her chores done, Stefa came and sat on my bed. 'Meesha, you know there's nothing pathologically wrong with you. The doctor noted some weakness of your heart muscle and what he calls "mild depression." As a nurse, I can tell you that these symptoms suggest you're overwhelmed with worry and self-reproach. And from what you've told me, I can understand how you feel.' She clasped her hands in her lap. 'I also thought it might help if I told you the story of another survivor: me. Promise you'll listen carefully?'

'Of course I'll listen,' I said. 'And thank you very much for spending time with me.'

Stefa shared that her parents and almost all her family had died during those ugly, brutal years. She and her brother, whose whereabouts she didn't now know, were the only ones who had survived. Before the war, Stefa's immediate family had lived in an exclusive area of Warsaw, where she attended a Catholic school. Soon after the Germans arrived in September 1939, they forced Jews to wear white armbands bearing the blue Star of David and began rationing food, as well as carrying out vicious public beatings and hangings.

In November 1940, the Germans constructed a ghetto in Warsaw and forced more than three hundred thousand Jews, one-third of the total population of the city, into an area consisting of only a few streets – a tiny fraction of the total area of the city. Conditions in the ghetto were unbearable, with multiple families packed into single apartments and given food rations gradually reduced to starvation levels.

Stefa and her family were luckier than others. Her father had managed to sell his business soon after the Germans invaded, and he had converted some of that money into gold coins, which enabled the family to barter for extra food.

Around the time when hunger, typhoid and other illnesses began to decimate those living in the ghetto, the Germans announced opportunities for young Jewish men to work in the East, where food was plentiful Hundreds signed up and were swiftly loaded onto trucks. When months passed with no word from any of these men, the rumours spread quickly – that they had been taken to the death camp Treblinka and gassed to death.

The few that had managed to escape eventually made their way back and confirmed people's worst fears. Some formed an underground group to develop connections with partisans outside the city. Stefa's parents decided that her brother should leave the ghetto. He joined the underground, disappeared, and was never heard from again.

A few months later, Stefa's father obtained false papers for her and got the name of a cloistered convent. Stefa looked Polish and, having spent ten years in Catholic school, behaved as a Polish woman. In January 1943, a few months before the ghetto was liquidated, Stefa escaped, leaving her parents, grandparents, and dozens of aunts, uncles, and cousins behind. She located the convent in a small village a few kilometres from Warsaw. During the next year and a half, she lived as if a nun.

At the convent, Stefa was assigned to study nursing in order to work in a neighbouring hospital. The war was raging, with the Germans in retreat, which meant the return of a lot of wounded soldiers. Nurses cared for the wounded, since many doctors had been mobilized.

'I picked up nursing really fast, and I love the profession,' she told me. 'Now, Meesha, I must go. Some other time I'll tell you the rest of the story.' Without meaning to sound ironic, she added, 'Go to sleep and have a good night's rest.' She caressed my face and left.

Stefa's story resonated within me. She, too, had lost her parents, relatives and all she had possessed. She had lived through more horrors than I had. Yet, she survived and was full of the will to live and even to prosper. Thanks to her counsel and example, I did sleep well that night. I woke in the morning refreshed, as if some of the burden had begun to lift from my shoulders.

Stefa continued to fill me with hope. 'Don't worry so much, Meesha,' she would say. 'If you and I survived, we are surely destined to live. Stop being a brooding philosopher. Live a little. Have a little fun.' A broad smile punctuated her advice.

A few days after Stefa had introduced herself, the doctor came to my bed to deliver good news. '*Herr* Kesler,' he said. 'I am discharging you today. You've made a good recovery, and I don't want to see you here, for a while anyway.'

'So, what was the matter with me, Herr Doctor?' I asked in broken German. My knowledge of Yiddish was the closest language to German I knew.

'I'll speak slowly, in German,' he said. 'It's the only language I know. Will that be all right?'

'Yes, Herr Doctor.'

'You had a bad cold, and you had a hard time recovering from it. Your heart developed some weakness and lost some of its muscle strength, probably as a result of years of trauma.' He smiled sympathetically. 'One pays a price for too much worry and grief.'

He'd read that I had lost my family and understood my complicated feelings about the tragedy. Excessive fear and anxiety affected one's vagus nerve, he explained, constricting blood circulation to the heart. It was a poor design of the system, resulting in a bitter irony: Just when the heart needed to pump faster to provide more blood to the brain and the body, so one could fight the causes of fear, the vagus nerve assured it did the opposite – this often being the cause of heart attacks in older people, or in those who die suddenly after losing a job or a life's mate.

'You're young, though,' he continued, 'so my hope is that the damage to your heart, in time, will heal. I wish you a good recovery and good luck.' He shook my hand and left.

Luba and I in Landsberg, March 1946.

He was a kind man, a decent man, and a German. I told myself not to forget this lesson: Good Germans existed after all.

***

After three weeks in the hospital, I rejoined Luba and Moniek. Later that first afternoon, I went into town, found a flower shop and bought a dozen red roses. I came back to our barrack, found a vase, filled it with water, and set the flowers inside. I then hid it in the bushes under our window. The next morning, I reclaimed the flowers and walked to the hospital to wait for Stefa.

Shortly after 8 a.m., she came out, still full of vivacity despite a night's work.

'Here, Stefa,' I said, greeting her. 'I brought you some flowers to thank you for all you have done for me.'

This startled her, and she accepted with a gentle reproach. 'You shouldn't have done it.' She embraced the bouquet as if it were a person and sniffed the roses. 'My, my, you must have spent a fortune. Did you inherit some money?' She took me by the hand, and it was as if an electric current surged through my body. I felt so close to her – enough that I was emboldened to ask if she would tell me the rest of her story.

Her warm grip of my hand tightened, and her face turned sad as she told me of how she left the convent and returned to Warsaw after the Russians had liberated it in the fall of 1944. Her family was gone, and so were all the Jews of the ghetto. Lonely, her spirit broken, Stefa returned to the apartment where her family had lived before the war and resumed her work as a nurse in a neighbouring hospital. She tried to make friends with the nurses in the hospital, yet felt estranged.

'They were not my friends,' she said. 'They couldn't be. The Poles could have saved countless numbers of Jews. They could have saved my parents. So many of them had stolen Jewish property and settled comfortably in Jewish homes. I no longer felt that this was my country.'

At the end of the war, miraculously, her brother found her. She was elated to have him back in her life, and he moved in with her. But he was a changed man. After his escape from the ghetto, he had lived in forests with other escapees. He had nearly starved to death and had almost been caught by the SS multiple times. Several of his comrades were caught and executed. He had lived like an animal, on the run, and, over the length of the war, he had lost his humanity.

One night he came to her bedroom and attempted to rape her. Stefa fought him off.

In the morning, she packed her things and left, renting a small apartment near the hospital. A young Polish doctor named Janusz took a liking to her and began to pursue her. She was lonely and gave in to his advances. They became lovers.

'But I was torn inside,' Stefa said. 'Janusz was good to me, and I suppose I loved him, but I felt disloyal to my parents, my family, and my people. As I walked the streets of Warsaw, I felt as if I was walking on their graves. The city was soaked with Jewish blood.' A few months later, in August 1945, she left Poland after hearing about the displaced persons camps in Germany. Beforehand, she told Janusz about her decision and that they must part. 'He was tearful and in pain, but he understood. He was a good man.'

'How did you manage to get to Germany?' I asked. 'We had a hard time crossing borders. Didn't you?'

Stefa explained that she still had her false papers, from when she had fled the ghetto. These made it easy for her to get to Czechoslovakia. From there, she travelled illegally to Austria, and in early September, she arrived at Landsberg, where she resumed her work as a nurse. A US Army major by the name of Irving Heymont immediately engaged her to assist him in his assignment to clean up the camp. She described to me the unbelievable squalor and despair of the survivors. The major was particularly concerned about sanitation and the threat of an epidemic. She became enmeshed in helping people come back to life – people who stared with vacant eyes and wore hopeless expressions that frightened her. She recalled sleepless nights and back-breaking work to put the camp into some semblance of normalcy, but she had received sweet rewards: the thankful glances of people whom she had put on the mend.

'So you see, Meesha,' she said, 'you're in good company. All the people here, not only you and me, have lived through hell. And we survived. We are alive, and that's what counts. We can't fix the past, so let's do something about the future – *our* future.'

I smiled and nodded.

'You want to come and meet my roommate?' she asked.

I obliged and we walked to her barrack. The room was familiar, the same as ours, with a partition separating Stefa's bed from that of her roommate.

'Hello, Basia!' She greeted a short, dark-haired woman in her thirties. 'Meet one of my patients.' Then she said to me, 'Come, Meesha, let's have some coffee. If I don't, I'll fall asleep.'

I introduced myself to Basia, and as we sat down, we began to chat.

'My friend here has told me that you have been mourning your parents,' Basia said.

I recounted my visit to the mass grave where my parents and all the Jewish townspeople lay.

'Our first job here at the camp, and earlier at St. Ottilien Hospital, was not so much to care for the physical condition of survivors,' Basia said, 'but rather their traumatized states of mind. They had lost their homes, their families, their roots, their stability. They truly didn't care to live. That made it difficult to treat them because we weren't trained for that.'

'You came here a couple of months after me. I never told you of the mess that we faced when I got here. I was immediately assigned to help the camp commander, United States Major Heymont. He's a wonderful man, as you well know, but he's tough. He took me by the hand and showed me the filthy bathrooms, with broken plumbing, plugged up toilets and feces on the floor, and the barracks covered with mold and dirt. He explained that he feared the unsanitary conditions would lead to an outbreak of disease, even an epidemic, in the camp if we didn't do something right away.'

'So how did you fix it?' I asked, eager to hear her reply.

'He assigned several people to help me, among them local German women. We started by getting down on our hands and knees to scrub the floors, first in the bathrooms, and then in the communal dining area. We also did our best to teach the survivors, who had been to hell and back, a minimum of sanitary practices. So day by day, week by week, we got the place cleaned up to Major Heymont's satisfaction.'

After sharing some buns and coffee with Stefa and Basia, I left, still ruminating on their comments about the terrible state of the camp and the survivors' mental and physical conditions. This alerted me to the probable difficulty I'd be facing when attempting to befriend people who had gone through hell. Their words opened my mind, prompting a new and profound appreciation for these two caring nurses and their devotion to improving the lives of people at the camp.

As the day wore on, thoughts of Stefa began to take hold. *I must see her again.*

In the evening I waited near her barrack, knowing that she would soon be leaving for work. Her eyes widened when she spotted me.

'I was out taking a walk,' I lied.

She laughed. 'The strange ways of young men to accost women on their way to work.'

As we walked toward the hospital, she told me of her correspondence with relatives in the United States. 'Maybe I'll get lucky and secure some papers to go to America. That would be something, wouldn't it, Meesha?'

'We're all waiting for miracles,' I replied. 'And my survival is proof that miracles do happen.'

All too soon we reached the infirmary.

'Well, good evening, Meesha,' Stefa said. 'I must go in to work. I hope to see you sometime when I'm not in such a hurry. Maybe the day after tomorrow – Sunday. Will you come?'

I nodded. 'I will, for sure.'

I walked back to my barrack, feeling as though I was floating above the ground – and away from the haunting past. The radio technician course had started a week earlier, and I had some catching up to do. The instructor was a young German in his thirties who lived in town, a kilometre or so away from the camp. He taught us how to assemble a radio from simple components, and how to improve it by adding new parts. We were also trained in the principles of radio transmission and basic electronics. The course was scheduled to last six months.

The twenty-two young Jewish men and women in the course were mostly survivors of death camps, with the exception of a few, like myself, who had spent the war years in the Soviet Union. Their stories, of barely having survived the camps, petrified me. True, I had heard and read much about the death camps and death marches, the gas chambers and crematories. But here were my classmates, my colleagues, speaking of the horrors at times in oddly matter-of-fact language. Indeed, their ordeals dumbfounded me, often leaving me tongue-tied in their presence. My struggles to survive with Luba were so puny, so superficial, compared with their suffering. I felt one step removed from their inconceivable pasts.

I did become close to Henry Kohen, an Auschwitz survivor who lost his entire family. We shared a zest for learning, hope for a better future, and a common goal to leave Europe – perhaps for Palestine.

As for his former years, Henry refused to dwell on them. 'My past is a cauldron of burning hell,' he said. 'I cannot bear to come close to it, lest it consume me.'

Henry, who was short with black hair and wore dark-rimmed glasses, was gentle and easy to be with. He mentioned having an extremely rich aunt in Florida who was trying to get him papers to come to the United States.

Though our experiences were different, our matching temperaments drew us together. Sometimes we dared to bemoan our fate of being confined to the camp, like a big jail. I confided to him that some of the survivors, with their wild, vacant eyes, frightened me. One, in particular, boasted of raping many German women after being liberated by the Red Army.

'You don't know a thing about the scene here in Landsberg before 1946,' Henry said. 'When I arrived here, the barracks' communal bathrooms were filthy – with faeces, and often vomit, covering the floor. People fought for a crust of bread, even though there was plenty to eat. They would push each other around with frightening hostility.'

Most often, however, Henry and I talked of the future – of a life renewed and dreams realized, and of new ones born. In time, I showed him my poems and shared with him versions of certain poems set to music.

The state of our lives – Moniek's, Luba's and mine – in the camp began to weigh heavily on my mind. We had no place to go, no hope of leaving. But we had enough to eat – certainly more than we'd had in the past five years – and we had a roof over our heads. Still, anger began to tear at me – anger at the Germans, at the Ukrainians and Poles, at a world that had known of Hitler's extermination of the Jews and had done nothing to stop it, and, finally, anger at a world intent on keeping us, the few survivors, locked up.

The news over the radio and in the press fueled my smoldering rage. Ernest Bevin, Great Britain's new secretary of state, was openly hostile toward Jews, and Britain was imposing strict limits on Jewish immigration to Palestine. The British navy intercepted boats with Jews heading to Palestine and diverted them to Cyprus, where they had set up internment camps.

When I shared my ire with Henry, I found him surprisingly level-headed about the situation. His view was that the British were acting out of fear, out of weakness. They had been losing one overseas possession after another because the war had impoverished them, making it difficult to hold on to their worldwide colonies. They were trying desperately to keep Jews out of Palestine so as not to alienate the oil-rich Arab states.

Henry's explanation made sense, and as the weeks and months went by, we dove into many more discussions on world order: the emergence of America as the sole superpower, the rising conflict between the Soviets and the United States, the rapidly developing civilian – and war-related – technology of atomic energy, and the emerging threat of nuclear confrontation.

Our hopes to go to the United States diminished, however. Jewish survivors – even those with visas – were being turned away daily by American consulates. Reports circulated in the Jewish press that the United

States had opened its gates instead to German scientists, engineers and even supervisors of death camps. It appeared that we, the survivors, would continue languishing in camps indefinitely.

I also continued seeing Stefa as often as possible. She was still assigned to the evening shift at the hospital, so I waited, often impatiently, to meet her on her way to work. Some evenings we visited the cafeteria together before her shift began.

She was bubbly, funny, cheerful and good to me, filling my days and nights with hopes and dreams. I would awake in the morning with the memory of seeing her the evening before, and waves of warmth and comfort would sweep over me, like the waves of the Ikva River on a hot summer day. More than that, I felt transported back to the woods of Dubno, where my family had spent a few summer vacations, dreaming I was alone with Stefa. I could almost touch her as she stretched under the pine trees – caressing her cheek, brushing her lips with mine.

I loved Stefa very much, but I was afraid of getting closer to her. She was a beautiful and confident woman, an accomplished nurse, and she came from a rich, presumably aristocratic, family. I, on the other hand, had no profession and only meager prospects for pursuing one. Surely I could be a weaver or a radio technician or a veterinary assistant, but those were no ways to support a family. I dreamed of becoming a scientist or an engineer, but how could I achieve either if I got married now?

Am I deserving of Stefa? I had my doubts, as I had with Sophie five years earlier. Despite my uncertainty, a small but strong flame of ambition kindled inside me.

∗∗∗

In early March, Luba announced she was pregnant. I was ecstatic. After so much tragedy, it was time to celebrate the anticipation of a new life. Though I tried to spend time with Luba, helping her with housekeeping chores, our relationship began to diminish in intensity. She and Moniek were drawing closer together, and I was beginning to feel left out of their plans and discussions. They talked often in hushed voices, and the more they separated themselves from me, the more alone I felt. Luba now thought of herself as a Perlman, meaning I truly was the only Kesler left.

And then another matter began to push us apart.

Moniek and his family belonged to the Bobover, an ultra-Orthodox Hasidic sect. It was named after the leader of the sect, who had come from

Bobov, a small town near Krakow. I was uncomfortable in that environment. Orthodox Judaism was built on a pillar of strict belief in a personal God – a God who predetermines the destiny of people, the destiny of each person, and is present in each person all the time.

'Was God present in Hitler when he committed his monstrous crimes?' I asked. 'Did God pre-determine the construction of gas chambers and crematoria to exterminate innocent people?'

I could not believe that.

Orthodox Judaism firmly claimed that God had chosen the Jewish people and favoured them with special love and attention. That notion did not square, and in fact seemed absurd to me, given the near annihilation of European Jewry.

Orthodox Jews believed in the sanctity of the Sabbath and its strict observance in accordance with laws codified more than fifteen hundred years ago, under living conditions drastically different from the present. They were stubbornly blind to the modern world around them.

'Don't touch the electric switches on the Sabbath,' Moniek scolded. 'Don't use the bicycle on the Sabbath. You can't carry anything on the street on the Sabbath.'

All his 'do this' and 'don't do that' irritated and stifled me. Life had been terribly constrained in the Soviet Union. Here, I finally felt free and unbound, primed to rebel against new yokes imposed on me, even in the name of religion.

My antipathy toward Orthodoxy led to a heated confrontation. Moniek had persuaded me to attend Bobover services on a Saturday that coincided with the beginning of a lunar month. On such occasions, traditional prayer books provided special prayers, including a phrase, '…because we and our fathers have sinned, our city was destroyed'. A bearded senior, and obviously revered, member of the congregation sermonized on the Sabbath. He singled out the quoted text for special comments: 'We and our fathers have sinned, in our own time as well, and God punished us with the tragedies that had befallen us.' He continued to excoriate those who had turned away from God. 'The redemption of all Jews will take place only when Jews return to God,' he concluded.

His sermon upset and offended me.

We returned to our apartment, where Moniek's cousins joined us for refreshments. In a voice loud enough for all to hear, I expressed my astonishment at the old man's linking the Holocaust with sins of the Jews.

'You're too critical and too quick to judge people,' Moniek shot back.

I answered that I did not think my parents were sinners, nor were the rest of the six million innocent Jews murdered by the Germans. I thought it both a crime and an offence to the memory of those who perished for anybody to make such an accusation.

'You must not question the ways of God,' one of the cousins said.

'A God who would send people to crematoria is no God for me!' Enraged, I stormed from the room, concluding that I could no longer stay with Luba and Moniek.

***

The DP camps were blessed with many visitors from America, as well as from Palestine, who encouraged us with lectures and promises. *Talk is cheap*, I often thought after listening to famous visitors speak of attempts to find us new homes. As it was, few US consulates were open, and they were flooded with applicants.

In late March, David Ben-Gurion, the head of the Jewish Agency in Palestine, came to Landsberg to deliver an address in the main hall. I arrived early, full of anticipation. I had read some of Ben-Gurion's speeches and pamphlets and regarded him as a man of action.

He was a short, chubby man, with shocks of white hair sprouting from the periphery of his ample, mostly bald, head. His facial features suggested someone of Ukrainian descent. 'I'm here to tell you that we will win our independence!' he exclaimed, his lively eyes dancing.

In contrast to his elf-like stature, Ben-Gurion's voice was that of a lion, and I listened to him with rapture.

He went on to assure us that the Jews in Palestine would defeat the British and build a new life, a new nation – one whose technological advances would be the envy of the world. One day the new Jewish homeland would become the Switzerland of the Middle East. 'We want all of you to join us in our struggle and in the building of our new nation. We want you young people to join the kibbutzim looking for volunteers here and at every DP camp. Join a kibbutz. Learn a trade. And in due time, we'll see you in our new land.'

That evening, I visited one of the kibbutzim, called Hashomer Hatzair. The kibbutz was one of many in the DP camps set up by the mother organizations in Palestine to attract and prepare young Jewish survivors for work in Palestine. It occupied nearly half a barrack and had more than a hundred young people. It was liberal in character, as it was sponsored by a left-of-centre political party in Palestine. After my experiences with ultra-Orthodox Jews, I concluded that the kibbutz suited me just fine. I registered and went back to Luba and Moniek to tell them of my decision.

'You don't have much respect for Judaism and your past,' Moniek said bitterly.

Luba stepped between us. 'Mekhel, we have good news to celebrate, so let's put aside this bickering.'

I was all too happy to avoid another quarrel. 'What is it?'

'Remember Aunt Leha in Uruguay?' Luba reminded me that our aunt, her husband Yoyne, two daughters, and her sister, Miriam, had left for Uruguay in 1933. They lived in Montevideo, where our aunt and uncle had a candy factory. Miriam was a practising nurse. Uruguay had no quotas on immigrants, and Aunt Leha wanted us to come there.

'That's unbelievable,' I said. 'How did she find us?'

'It's I who found them,' Luba answered with pride. 'I wrote to them a month or so ago, and now I have an answer.' She snatched the letter from the table and handed it to me.

It was written in Yiddish and was genuinely warm and welcoming.

'They really want us to come!' After a moment, I asked, 'What about Eva and the cousins – will they be going to Uruguay as well? The letter doesn't mention them.'

'They want to wait for visas to go to the United States,' Moniek replied. 'The Bobover rebbe (the chief of the Hasidim from Bobov) is arranging for them to emigrate.'

'You'll come with us, right?' Luba asked me.

'I've just joined the kibbutz,' I replied, feeling torn. 'I don't know where it will lead me. I may be going to Palestine soon.'

Sadness overtook me. Luba and Moniek were leaving. The Perlmans, too, would soon be gone. My loneliness made a sudden and powerful return.

The next morning, I gathered my few belongings and walked to the kibbutz, where they assigned me to a room with three other young men. It was a bit crowded, but it turned out that we didn't spend much time in our rooms.

All of us were enrolled in training courses given by either ORT or the kibbutz. Most afternoons we spent working on the fifty-acre farm adjoining the barracks. The farm, appropriated from a high-ranking Nazi official, became the focus of our training – to prepare for work on a farm in Palestine. Tilling the ground with limited farm machinery, planting seeds, and weeding proved back-breaking work. The dream of cultivating our own homeland in Palestine, however, sweetened my slumber.

In the evening, we shared our meals in a big hall. Each of us took turns preparing or serving meals. Friday evenings were special, the big hall decorated with flowers and plastic tablecloths, and a bottle of wine on each table. Compared with the privations we had suffered during the war, the meals were sumptuous, typically consisting of chicken with vegetables, salad and dessert. The evening started and ended with fiery Zionist songs, and we always had a speaker – most often one of us, but sometimes a visiting dignitary from the United States or Palestine. Thus, we welcomed and celebrated the Sabbath, not with prayer or religious ritual, but with excitement and joy. We were drawn together by common experience, common hopes, and common dreams. It felt good to be alive.

The Passover holiday on 16 April filled me with pride and happiness I hadn't known since before fleeing Poland. I had been writing poems and songs, some full of sadness from the past, but others ringing with Jewish nationalist fervor.

For the first night's seder, I read a poem I had composed. I was followed by the famed poet, H. Leivik, who was visiting the camp. Leivik was a writer for *Der Tog* (a New York Yiddish-language daily newspaper). He took my poem and promised to have it published in the paper. I was excited and proud. At the seder, we read from the Manischewitz *Haggadah*, a free publication distributed by the kosher winemaker. This took me back to long hours spent at home reading the *Haggadah*, with Dad adding commentary. At this seder, however, there was little reading from the text and instead a lot of singing and commentaries by survivors. The comments and speeches ended with strong commitments to life, and affirmations of being free in our new homeland. Yes, it was a miracle to have survived, and it was wonderful to be free.

In truth, though, we were not entirely free.

A few days later, I met up with Stefa at the hospital cafeteria and told her about the exhilarating feeling I'd had at Passover and of my encounter with the famous poet Leivik.

Then, in a sudden change of mood, I expressed my anger at being locked up with nowhere to go. I told her of Luba and Moniek's plan to travel to Uruguay and how they wanted me to go with them. I had even begun to take Spanish lessons, just in case. But my heart wasn't in it. Uruguay was a wonderful country to offer asylum to Jews, but it was small and had little to offer. I would probably end up working on a farm. 'What are your plans, Stefa?' I asked.

My friend Stefa, May 1946

'I'm getting impatient waiting as well,' she answered with a sigh. 'I don't know when the United States will open its doors to us. Meanwhile, there is no way to apply for a visa, even if I receive the papers from Aunt and Uncle. Let's talk more about it. How about Sunday?'

I planted a gentle kiss on her cheek. 'I'll see you then.'

***

That Sunday, after we'd eaten our small breakfast, Stefa said, 'I've got an idea, Meesha. I'll prepare a couple of sandwiches, and we'll go for a hike in the woods. Do you like that idea?'

'I love it.'

Soon we were on our way. I held her hand as we strolled, and it felt good. Stefa was cheerful as usual, telling me funny stories and exploding with laughter as she told them. The day was beautiful, the sky blue and cloudless. The pathways in the woods were bordered by new blossoms and foliage – new life.

When we reached a large clearing with fresh grass still covered in beads of dew, Stefa opened her bag and lifted out a blanket. 'Help me and then let's rest.'

When we lay down, Stefa turned toward me and put her hand on my cheek.

'You look lovely,' I said.

She smiled. 'Thank you. I needed to hear that.' Her expression turned serious. 'I'm so often lonely and sad. You remember I told you I had a lover once, and that I loved him too? I experienced several months of happiness, but fear of innate Polish hatred against our people tore us apart.'

I nodded, touched by her openness. But I was also taken aback. Stefa had lived with another man – a Polish man. My mind drifted to Sophie, who was much like Stefa, but so much closer to my ideal, her image and memory unspoiled by the horrors of war.

Stefa turned to me. 'Do you like me, Meesha?'

'Yes, I do,' I confessed. 'Very much.'

She hesitated, and then said, 'Do you *love* me?'

'I do, Stefa, with all my heart. I think of you, dream of you. I want to be with you. You're beautiful, and you have a wonderful soul.'

'Then why are you so shy with me?'

When I didn't answer, she blurted sharply, 'Meesha, have you ever loved another woman?'

I started to tell her about Sophie.

'I don't think you understand me,' she said a bit irritably. 'Have you ever had sex with a woman? I mean, have you heard about the birds and the bees?'

The sarcasm in Stefa's voice could not be missed, and I was taken by surprise. I had never seen her angry. Feeling as though I'd been slapped in the face, I remained silent.

Hastily, Stefa got to her feet. 'Let's go back.'

I helped her fold and pack the blanket, and we started off. Stefa was quiet all the way to her apartment, and I knew she was hurt and feeling rejected.

After we parted, I berated myself – for behaving like a fool, like a boy, just as I had in the army.

You'd better grow up, I told myself.

Toward the end of the week, I ran into Stefa, but she was in a hurry and hardly spoke to me. Saturday evening, I saw her again, sitting at a table in the cafeteria with Basia and a young man who wasn't familiar to me. Stefa was animated, laughing with abandon. When I approached them, she didn't bother to introduce me, so I walked away, feeling hurt.

A few days later, again in the cafeteria, Basia approached me. 'Can I talk to you?'

We stepped outside and sat on a wooden bench near the entrance.

'I want to understand what's going on between you and Stefa,' Basia said. 'She's a dear friend to me, and she feels hurt that you rejected her. You've been seeing each other for nearly half a year. She expected that the two of you would become intimate, that you would show you really love her.' She tilted her head. 'Don't you love her, Meesha?'

'I do love Stefa, as much as I have ever loved anyone. I admire her – worship her.'

'Okay, then.' Basia regarded me with open, inquisitive eyes. 'Have you ever loved a woman…sexually?'

With the subject finally out in the open, I surprised myself and freely responded, 'No, I've never made love to a woman before.'

She nodded. 'How old are you?'

'Twenty-one.'

'You know, I'm a nurse. And I've found most men your age to be aggressive sexually, and often promiscuous too.' She leaned in, keeping her voice low. 'Are you attracted to men?'

I reared back. 'Absolutely not! You may be a nurse, but you've misdiagnosed the problem here.' I explained that I came from a small shtetl where relationships were forever, where love was more than just sex, and, moreover, one did not enter a sexual relationship lightly.

Basia, listening intently, scooted closer to me. I could feel my face growing hot as I expressed to her the warmth and joy I felt being in love with Stefa.

She smiled – almost mockingly, it seemed. 'Meesha, you're a romantic.'

'And what's wrong with that?'

'You've read too much poetry,' she said, giving a dismissive wave. 'Come down to earth. Be realistic. Stefa is a woman in her prime. She needs love and affection, and physical love is an important part of that.' Basia's expression grew serious. 'You know she has known another man.'

The blood returned to my face. 'I do.'

'She has known the joy and ecstasy of love, whereas you have not.'

'I suppose I have a lot to learn.'

'I'd say,' Basia said. 'Sexual love can bind you together and transport you to a world of happiness you haven't yet known or imagined.'

My friend Stefa and her friend Basia, May 1946.

'I appreciate your insights,' I said, growing tired of the lecture. 'But for the present, I'm more concerned with how I might someday support a wife and family. As it is, I fear we might all rot in this camp. I'm not sure whether to wait with the hope of one day going to Palestine, or if I should go ahead with my sister and her husband to Uruguay. I haven't a clue what Stefa is thinking about any of this, and while I love her very much, I don't want to hurt her, or myself, by being impulsive.'

Basia ignored my attempt to shift the subject. 'You remember that young man at our table last Saturday?'

I felt a stab to the heart. 'Yes.'

'He admires Stefa as well, and if you keep insisting on a purely romantic, platonic love – whatever your reasons – you'll lose her. Stefa loves and respects you, but she desires a mature relationship.' Basia stood to go and set a hand on my shoulder. 'Meesha, you must grow up and start making decisions. The sooner the better.'

A week passed.

I kept thinking about Basia's words and regretting that I hadn't been more forthcoming with Stefa, that I'd disappointed her. Toward the end of the week, I ran into her, but her warm smile and wink were gone. She was in a hurry to get to work, she said, so we didn't talk long.

That evening, a pain both bitter and sweet sprouted within me. Sweet for the love I still had for Stefa, yet bitter for the realization that I was losing her. I grew angry with myself. I should have understood what she wanted – needed – from me. I shouldn't have let her go.

Stop playing the romantic saint, I chastised myself. *Be a man!*

Guilt, remorse, and shame consumed me. Sleep that night was fitful, at best.

***

A few mornings later, while eating breakfast in the cafeteria, I was astounded to see Joseph Gitman. We embraced as would brothers, tears flowing down our cheeks.

I invited him to sit with me. 'How did you get here?' I asked.

'With great difficulty.' Joseph told me that after leaving Dubno, where we had last seen each other, he traveled roads infested with Ukrainian guerillas to Czechoslovakia, where he arrived in the spring of 1946. He stayed in Prague for a couple of months, and then entered the US Occupation Zone. 'So here I am,' he said, taking a sip of coffee. 'And where have you been?'

I recounted to Joseph our travels and travails of the past half year, and of our lives in the camp, including Luba's pregnancy and my hope of going to Palestine.

Joseph said he planned to wait in Landsberg while his relatives in New York secured him papers to emigrate to the United States.

As our conversation progressed, I told him about my love for Stefa and my despair at losing her due to my reluctance concerning physical intimacy.

'So you have not had sex with anybody before?'

I smiled sheepishly. 'I almost did – once.' I described my encounters with Mahdu, and how I had once ejaculated while necking in her dorm room.

'And then?'

'Then I had to say goodbye.' I shrugged. 'I'm sure we would have had sex eventually, had I stayed. But my feelings for Stefa are different from those I had for Mahdu. They're more transcendent somehow, more idealized.' I pushed my empty tray aside. 'I feel so stupid.'

'You're not stupid, Mekhel,' Joseph said. 'I can understand your reluctance. The way you broke down at our parents' grave. Such trauma leaves deep scars. You're probably still in mourning.' He explained that certain animals, such as cheetahs, don't procreate in captivity. 'Being cooped up here in this camp, you're probably also depressed.' He patted my hand. 'Give it time, Mekhel. Don't rush things.'

I respected Joseph, but his words were less than convincing. Luba had grown so distant. And now I'd lost Stefa. I'd never felt more alone.

∗∗∗

Toward the end of May 1946, my ORT school travelled by truck to the countryside for a belated Lag B'Omer (an upbeat, festive holiday) picnic. As our driver joyfully passed another truck loaded with ORT students, prompting much singing and banter, I sat quietly to myself. Pangs of love tightened my chest: I lost Stefa, a wonderful woman.

The idea of remaining in this oppressive camp – this jail – forever enraged me. I became depressed.

Doesn't anybody give a damn about us?

I stood abruptly, driven by a force I couldn't contain, and approached the right side of the truck, prepared to jump to the other. The strong hands of two classmates pulled me back and pushed me down.

'Are you stupid? You could have been killed!'

I recognized Henry Orenstein's strong, commanding voice. A survivor of Auschwitz, Henry dominated every discussion, silencing anyone who dared to challenge his views.

I managed to calm down, and an hour later, we took out our sandwiches and held a celebratory repast.

'Meesha, why did you do it?' Henry Kohen sat down beside me. 'Did you want to commit suicide?'

I explained that I was sad, having broken things off with Stefa, whom Henry had met and liked.

'You'll find another woman,' he said. 'Your time will come. Don't worry.'

***

At the end of the first week of July 1946, bad news reached us at the ORT.

The previous month, one of our classmates, Peter, having given up hope of ever joining his relatives in the United States or travelling to Palestine, returned to his hometown of Kielce. While here, he had often complained of feeling no different than he had while in Auschwitz – except for the ovens and gas chambers. He was angry and frustrated – justifiably so.

Sadly, on 4 July 1946, a pogrom erupted in Kielce, resulting in the violent deaths of fifty Jews who had dared to return home, Peter being one of them.

We mourned and we cried, while affirming our determination never to return to Poland. There was only one place for us: a new home in Palestine.

News of the Kielce killings devastated me. The Poles had no use for Jewish survivors of the genocide. The memory of the Ukrainian who had answered our door in Dubno, waving his pitchfork and screaming, 'Get out, you dirty Jews!' flashed through my mind. Like the Ukrainians, the Poles had stolen Jewish property and would kill any Jew who returned to claim what was his.

My blood boiled. *Nobody wants us!*

The British slammed on us the doors to Palestine, lest our presence there offend the Arabs. The United States was courting the Germans to stave off the Soviet threat to the rest of Europe. The Germans I had met inside and outside of the camp pleaded innocence to the barbarism they had wrought. The UNRRA officials often spoke of love and empathy, but they had little more to offer beyond what a jailer would to a prison inmate.

It was at about this time – again, in the cafeteria – I noticed a familiar new arrival.

Osher Balaban, accompanied by a visibly pregnant blonde woman, embraced me as a brother. 'Meet my bride, Zhenya,' he said.

I was overjoyed to see the man who had made it possible for me to escape the Soviet army. Osher reminded me that he had mentioned Zhenya, the nurse who had tended to him as he lay helplessly wounded in a Stalingrad hospital, when we had seen him in Samarkand. They had been together ever since.

He expressed his and Zhenya's eagerness to leave the blood-soaked continent of Europe to help build a new country in Palestine. He also told me of the tragic loss of his older brother in the battle of Stalingrad.

I recounted Luba's marriage and told him of Joseph Gitman, whom he had known in Dubno. Soon we connected with Joseph, and with Henry Kohen, and the four of us went on to meet often to discuss world affairs, our disappointment of being stuck in the camp and our hope of going to Palestine.

My classmates in the Radio Technician course at Landsberg, June 1946. I am in the top row, second from left.

Meanwhile, the ORT course came to an end, and we celebrated the occasion with our mentor, Dr. Jacob Oleiski, a concentration camp survivor and the head of ORT training in the Landsberg camp. He was a trained agronomist who had worked for ORT in Lithuania before the war. His graduation address emboldened us to continue productive work on the camp's farm in order to prepare ourselves for fruitful lives in Palestine.

Dr. Oleiski, along with other officials from UNRRA, pumped a new fighting spirit into me, and I began to work feverishly on the farm. I also wrote many letters to the editor of the Jewish newspaper, and submitted some poems as well. In addition, I composed several songs that friends and many others in the camp came to sing.

Several days after graduation, Joseph met me with shocking news. A huge explosion had rocked the King David Hotel in Jerusalem on 22 July, killing ninety and injuring dozens more. The hotel housed Britain's administrative headquarters in Palestine. A terrorist group called the Irgun, a militant underground Zionist organization, claimed responsibility.

'This is the beginning of the end of British occupation!' Joseph told me with excitement. He further explained that in the process of winning the war, England had emptied its treasury and was unable to maintain its worldwide empire. Its troubles in Palestine were but a harbinger of Britain's desperate need to shrink its holdings.

In early August, the kibbutz was preparing to leave for Palestine. We were told to bid farewell to family and friends, so one evening I went to say goodbye to Luba and Moniek. It proved painful and not without tears.

Five years of wandering, of fighting for survival, of joint suffering and worries, flooded my mind. My parents' appeal to me to take care of Luba rang in my ears. Luba's baby was due in a month. I was torn with doubt and worry.

Luba cried as she embraced me. 'I hope we will see each other again,' she said when she finally let me go.

Trucks were waiting near the kibbutz to take us to Hamburg, where we would board a ship to Palestine. We were packed and ready to leave. The early morning hours ticked away. Then, at five o'clock, the leader of the kibbutz announced that our trip had been cancelled. The British had intercepted the ship that was to take us from Hamburg to Palestine and sequestered it in Cyprus. Devastated by the news, we embraced each other and bewailed our fate.

For me, the incident prompted the return of dark thoughts. The world had abandoned us. We would rot in this camp forever, amidst our worst enemies. We had given so much to the world: Moses, Einstein, Freud. We had given birth to monotheism, which the Christians and Muslims had appropriated and corrupted before deciding to rid themselves of us altogether.

Overcome by loneliness, I thought of Stefa. *Why did I abandon her?*

My despondency, however, was short-lived. The hard knocks of the past five years had taught me to persevere, to summon my reserves and fight on. Instinctively, I burst out with 'Hatikvah', our hymn of hope, and everyone joined me. Our voices reverberated throughout the large, shabby hall until, exhausted and bleary-eyed, we sat for a meager breakfast.

Later that day, I visited Luba and Moniek. Luba greeted me with her usual cheerful embrace. But as she did so, I could hardly reach her face, her swollen belly coming between us.

My! I thought. *She's going to give birth soon. How happy she must be.* I hesitated to spoil her mood, and yet, I couldn't hold it back. I told her how the British had diverted our ship, and how I wasn't sure if we'd ever get to Palestine. I fought tears as my bitterness unfolded. 'Maybe I should have stayed home with Mom and Dad and accompanied them to the killing fields.' I described again the scene of the mass grave on the outskirts of Dubno that haunted me still.

Moniek appeared suddenly. 'Mekhel, stop talking such foolishness!' he shouted. 'Do you know the story of the wife of Lot, Abraham's nephew? She looked back at Sodom and turned into a pillar of salt. That's what's going to happen to you if you keep looking at the past and cursing your fate.'

'We must live!' Luba exclaimed. 'We must go on living!'

I quieted as she prepared a simple lunch on the small, round, electric hot plate.

She then read to me the latest letter from our aunt in Uruguay. 'So, you see, there is hope. Uruguay is a small country. And Moniek's talents will surely single him out and provide plenty of opportunities for us to settle down and prosper.'

I promised Luba and Moniek that if ever I made it to the States I would secure papers for them and the baby to join me there.

***

Soon, life's rhythm resumed. I opened my eyes to the many cultural events the camp offered. There were lectures aplenty by highly educated people, some of whom served as editorial writers for the main local Jewish newspaper. The camp had organized a small orchestra that performed many popular songs, as well as short excerpts from the classical repertoire, with singers invited to participate. I ventured to offer a couple of my new songs, to great applause.

While onstage, I noticed a striking young woman in the front row regarding me intently.

Helen, with her dark complexion, glossy black hair and delicate nose that looked as if sculpted by an artist, attracted me immediately, and we began seeing each other.

Something about her, however, alerted me to beware. Although she professed to like me, she was decidedly distant, as if holding something back. A couple weeks into our courtship, while sitting together outside her barrack, she said she wished for me to hear her story of survival.

She pursed her soft, lush, red lips. 'Maybe you will not like me so much after you hear what I have to tell you.'

My ears perked up. I had by now heard many frightening stories of camp survivors.

She straightened and her face turned serious, her dark eyes staring straight into mine.

Upon her arrival at Auschwitz, she told me, Josef Mengele, aka the Angel of Death, had singled her out to live. Soon she found herself at Birkenau, and was later transported to another camp, where she ended up in its bordello, dispensing pleasure to SS guards. She forced herself to please each of them as best she could, for she knew many attractive inmates who had dared protest ended up in the gas chamber. The ordeal sapped her of all feeling, rendering her numb to all male advances. She wanted me to know this, since she considered me innocent and likely chaste. She understood pain and did not want to hurt me. I listened to her in rapt silence, at one point grabbing her cold hand and caressing it.

When I moved to embrace her, she did not reciprocate.

She was right. I did not understand – could never understand the depth of suffering that survivors of the concentration camps had endured and how the cruelty of their situation had diminished their own humanity and ability to love.

Shortly thereafter, Helen and I parted.

***

In a few weeks, I'd be completing the radio technician course. But what then? Would I practise what I learned among the mortal enemies of my people?

Unthinkable, I thought. *Unacceptable.*

Luba and Moniek were ready to leave, but because Luba was expecting in a few weeks, they decided to wait. They were still urging me to go with them, but I could not get excited about Uruguay. Besides, I wanted to stand on my own, not be dependent on Luba or my relatives. I was considering studying engineering in Germany while waiting my turn to go to Palestine. I had even visited the Technische Hochschule München and took an entrance exam.

A week or so later, the institute confirmed my acceptance, and I moved into one of the dorms and began my studies. I felt revitalized, as if reborn.

Later in September, I spotted a notice on the bulletin board that B'nai B'rith-Hillel was offering scholarships for qualified DP students. If interested, one should apply through the UNRRA office. The ad intrigued me, and I could think of no reason not to take a chance. I sent in copies of my meagre documents and waited. Two weeks later, I received a notice from UNRRA requesting that I take a university entrance exam.

On Simchat Torah, Luba gave birth to a baby boy. I immediately returned to Landsberg, feeling as if the child were my own. Eight days later, we celebrated the infant's circumcision, a joyous event shared by all of Moniek's friends and relatives. Amid plenty of food, singing, and dancing, the entire community expressed delight.

In late October, after returning to the university, I received a letter inviting me to meet with Colonel Jospe, head of the local UNRRA office. I opened the door to Colonel Jospe's office full of anticipation. The colonel looked to be in his mid-forties with dark hair and distinct Semitic features. When he stood, I found that he was not much taller than I.

'Welcome, Michael,' he said, shaking my hand. 'Please, sit.'

He asked me what languages I spoke, and to my surprise, he agreed to speak to me in Yiddish. As we spoke, he observed me intently, as if trying to read my thoughts. He wanted to know my background and asked what I wanted to do with my life. I told him that I wanted to be a scientist or an engineer.

'I bear good news for you, then. You passed your college admission test with flying colours. You look to me like a bright, serious young man. So Hillel's representatives in this country have selected you as a young, capable Jewish DP to go to the United States and fulfil your well-deserved aspirations for professional studies.'

The blood rushed to my face. 'I'm delighted to hear that,' I said excitedly.

'I'm more than delighted,' the colonel continued, 'to tell you that you've been accepted to Colby College in Waterville, Maine.'

I hesitated, embarrassed by my ignorance. 'What is a...college?'

He explained that it was much like a university, though with fewer departments.

'And Waterville is where exactly?'

He opened a map of the United States and smoothed it out on his desk, pointing to the state of Maine and the town. 'You know,' he said, 'I believe the climate in Maine is close to that of Poland, where you come from.' He then described the Hillel scholarship and emphasized that it would cover all tuition and some living expenses for four years.

There was one caveat, however. American consulates in Germany had stopped accepting applications for visas from Jews. I would first have to go to France and remain there for at least six months to establish legal residency. Only then would I be able to travel to the States.

'Will that be acceptable to you?' Jospe asked.

I smiled broadly. 'More than acceptable. Thank you.'

After explaining that his secretary would arrange for my trip from Munich to Paris, Colonel Jospe stood and shook my hand. 'Mazel tov!'

I left his office, drunk with joy. At last, the beginning of a new life.

Yet, I could not help but feel some disappointment about not going to Palestine. I had grown up with the dream of someday redeeming the land of ancient Israel. The sarcastic taunting of my Polish classmates before the war – 'Jew, go to Palestine!' – only reinforced those dreams. Zionist literature, teachers in the Hebrew school, lectures, the press, and all sorts of after-school activities strengthened my belief that Palestine belonged to the Jews and that I belonged there. The Holocaust confirmed to me that living as a minority in foreign countries subjected the Jews to the whims of dictators and killers. Palestine and only Palestine, I was convinced, would provide a safe haven for us, the remnants of a persecuted people.

I felt comfortable in the kibbutz, my adopted home. The spirit of Hashomer Hatzair, accompanied by daily and weekend routines, made me feel as if I were living and working in a virtual Palestine, helping to build a Jewish national home. I was prepared and eager to go to Palestine, but, once again, the world conspired against us. Meanwhile, I had been given an unbelievable opportunity to go to the United States and study.

Maybe this is right. Let me first learn a profession, then I will go and be a productive citizen of the new Jewish nation.

This would require moves to France, the United States and finally to Palestine, but I had spent so many years catching trains from one place to the next that this did not deter me.

***

Where Shall I Go?

© Copyright February 2008, Don Bloom, E. Brunswick, N.J.

The next morning, I went to the registrar's office at the Technische Hochschule München and announced I was leaving for the States, showing him the admission letter from Colby College. He said the university would send me my transcripts, and then congratulated me and wished me well. I continued on to the dormitory, packed my few belongings, and caught a train to Landsberg.

Luba was surprised to see me. 'What brings you here, Mekhel?' she asked. I joyfully embraced her.

'I came to say goodbye!' I exclaimed.

'Where are you going?'

I explained to Luba that I got a scholarship to study in America. 'Not so fast, my brother. You make my head swim,' she said. 'So where are you going to be, my big shot brother? And when are you leaving?'

'Don't get so excited,' I said as I told her that I could not go directly and had to swing around Paris for a few months.

She looked happy, but confided that, a month earlier, she'd had to go to the hospital to have a cyst on her breast removed. 'Nothing to worry about, Mekhel,' she assured me. 'Just a little cyst, and it was not cancerous. I am one hundred per cent all right.'

I did worry, though, and I felt guilty that I hadn't been there in her time of need.

The boy, now three months old, was sleeping peacefully in the corner of the room. From my subjective point of view, he was the most beautiful child on earth.

'Where's Moniek?' I asked.

'He's trying to patent a new design on the electric shaver,' she said. 'Did you know that many Orthodox men didn't want to grow beards but were

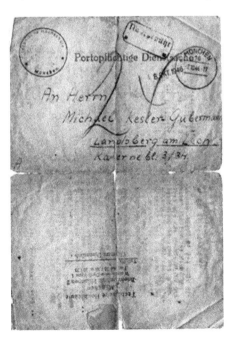

Herrn/Fr1...

Betreff: Zulassung zum Hochschulstudium.

Laut Entschließung des Bayer.Staatsministeriums für Unterricht und
Kultus vom 27.8.1946 Nr.VI 42286 und vom 16.9.1946 Nr.VI 42088 können - bei Erfüllung der sonstigen Voraussetzungen in politischer
Beziehung usw. - im Wintersemester 1946/47 zum Studium an der Technischen Hochschule München **n i c h t** zugelassen werden:
1.) Bewerber, die das 35.Lebensjahr vollendet haben (können grund-
    sätzlich nicht als Erstsemester zugelassen werden),
2.) Bewerber, die nach dem 1.7.1925 geboren sind,
3.) Bewerber, die im Jahre 1946 ein normales Reifezeugnis erwar-
    ben haben (nicht also Teilnehmer an Sonderkursen und Förde-
    rungskursen), und
4.) (aus räumlichen Gründen) Bewerber, von außerbayerischen Län-
    dern (soweit sie nicht schon früher an der Technischen Hoch-
    schule München studiert haben.
Diese Bewerber (ausgenommen Ziff.1) haben nur dann Aussicht auf
Zulassung zum Studium im Wintersemester 1947/48 (planmäßiger Be-
ginn für die Studierenden der Naturwissenschaften und der technischen Fachrichtungen), wenn sie nachweisen, daß sie beim Wieder-
aufbau der Hochschule eine lang beschäftigt waren. Dieser Ein-
satz bei den Instandsetzungs- bei Wiederaufbauarbeiten der Technischen Hochschule München ist bei einer mit der Durchführung der
Arbeiten beteiligten Baufirma zu leisten. Anmeldungen nimmt das
Baubüro der Technischen Hochschule München entgegen, das auch die
Einstellung vermittelt.

München, den 1.Oktober 1946
Der Rektor der Technischen Hochschule

**Cover and inside of record from the
Technischen Hochschule of Munich,
October 1946**

---

prohibited from using razor blades to shave them off? But then some rabbis,
apparently, declared that it was all right to use *electric* shavers.'

'So that's why he has been working so hard on a design?'

Luba nodded. 'With any luck, he'll be able to patent it and make some
money. We shall see.'

'And what about Uruguay?' I asked. 'When will you be leaving?'

'We decided to postpone until spring, until Nathan grows a bit older and
easier to manage.' She gestured to the table in the middle of the room. 'Sit
down, Mekhel. I'll prepare some food. Moniek should be home soon too.'

'Actually, I was hoping to run over to the ORT and find out what
happened to my classmates. I should be back in an hour or two.'

A few minutes later, at the ORT office, I learned that most of my
classmates were gainfully employed, mostly in Munich. Henry Kohen
and two others were working here in Landsberg. Later, I stopped at the
kibbutz and discovered that most of its members were still there. Rather
than pursuing work or careers, they were waiting, impatiently, to go to
Palestine.

The evening meal with Luba and Moniek was filled with convivial
banter. I shared my dream of studying to be an engineer, while Moniek,
with enthusiasm, told of his plans to market his electric shaver, as well as
develop other ideas he had in mind.

© Copyright February 2008, Mark Sherman, Delmar, CA.

I tried to be happy, but I was sad. It would be so difficult to part. *Will I see Luba, Moniek and my little nephew again?*

'Luba,' I said the next morning, 'I want to ask you a favour. I didn't have a chance to say goodbye to Joseph Gitman. Would you please tell him that I am sorry, and that I hope we will see each other in Paris? Last I heard, he was going to the States and would probably be going through Paris.'

Then I embraced Luba, shook hands with Moniek, kissed Nathan, and left.

Another chapter of my life closed as I headed back to Munich. Later that afternoon, I took the train to Paris.

15

Parisian Interlude and Beyond

I arrived in Paris on the morning of 30 November 1946, travelling under the sponsorship of the Joint Distribution Committee. A Joint staff member, Jacques Kaufman, met me at the Orsay train station and introduced himself in French. Immediately, he noticed my language difficulty and removed from his pocket a Polish-French dictionary, expressing his hope that it would help me get by.

Jacques, a smiling and jovial man in his twenties, ushered me to the metro station, where we boarded a train to Belleville Station. A short distance away was Passage de la Croix, a narrow alley in the twentieth arrondissement, or district, at the end of which stood a dilapidated old hotel – Number 5.

Jacques registered me with the concierge, and the three of us climbed the steps to the second floor. We walked down a long, dark hall, until the concierge stopped and opened a door to a small room. She handed me the keys, showed me how to use the little gas stove in the corner, and ducked out.

The room seemed more a prison cell, roughly five feet wide by eight feet long, with cracked walls, peeling paint, and a small, dirty window at the end. A narrow bed sat to the right of the door. Under the window, opposite the sink and the little stove, stood a café-style table with two chairs.

I set my satchel on the bed, and Jacques and I sat down at the little table. He apologized in a mixture of Yiddish and French for the poor accommodations, explaining that the twentieth arrondissement was the poorest in Paris. 'The city is built like a spiral,' he explained, 'with the first arrondissement, at the centre, being the richest, followed by less well-to-do areas, and ending here, where mostly blue-collar people live.'

He gave me the address of a radio repair shop, where the Joint had found a job for me, as well as the address for a local cafeteria to eat my evening meals. After giving me a week's supply of meal tickets and some pocket money for daily expenses, he shook my hand enthusiastically and bade me good luck.

Thus, I had been initiated as a Parisian.

Later that first day, I travelled to the shop owned by a French Jew, François Gilbert, who fortunately spoke a bit of Yiddish.

François spent some time questioning me about where I'd been during the war, then volunteered that he, too, had nearly perished before running away and hiding with a fellow Frenchman in the Pyrénées.

'I'm sure you know the trade well,' he said, after reviewing my transcripts. 'The Germans are good, precise teachers. However, you'll have to be able to communicate with the customers before I can use you.' He told me about a school nearby, called Alliance Française, which taught French to foreigners. He wanted me to enroll, offering to pay the tuition in addition to my regular salary.

I thanked him profusely.

He stepped into his office and soon reemerged with a broad smile. 'You're in luck, Mr. Kesler. There's a course scheduled to begin tomorrow. See you in six weeks.'

***

I took the metro back to Belleville, found a small grocery store, and bought some food and other necessities before returning to my little cell. The next morning, I hunted down the Alliance Française. For the next six weeks, I immersed myself in yet another language necessary for my survival, studying from early morning and through the day. Evenings, I had dinner in the cafeteria that served mostly refugees like me.

I took a liking to the French language, which was soft, sonorous and beautiful to enunciate. I also loved the literature I was being exposed to, especially the passion for social justice, equality, and enlightenment found in the writings of Hugo, Zola, and Balzac, which stirred me with hope. *Maybe there is a future for man, after all – a just and peaceful future.*

In mid-January I returned to the shop, where François wasted no time engaging me in conversation. 'You're a fast learner,' he said, impressed with my progress. 'I think you're ready to start.'

Armed with my new language skills, I was prepared for the repair and sales work François had hired me to do. The hours were much shorter than those I'd forced on myself while studying French. At five in the evening, my day at the shop came to a close, and with two hours to kill before dinner, I explored the streets of Paris.

From the vast Champs Élysées and majestic Arc de Triomphe, to the expansive Place de la Concorde and the architecturally striking Eiffel Tower

A picture of me in Paris, March 1947.

– not to mention its endless parks – the famed 'City of Lights' did not disappoint, filling me with admiration.

Where does so much genius – for architecture, city planning, construction, and aesthetics – come from? I wondered. *And how did it all culminate here in Paris?*

Gradually, I became familiar with the various concert halls and musical events in the city. Standing-room-only tickets came cheap, and I took full advantage, particularly on weekends. After the war, Paris became the mecca of the artistic world. I had been exposed to many of the musical classics in Germany via the radio, but this was the first time I'd seen and heard famous conductors, composers and soloists in person. I listened carefully to the pure awesomeness of Beethoven's *Eroica*, the urgency of his *Fifth*, and delighted in the cosmic reaches of the *Ninth*, which, in my opinion, was the most exultant musical piece ever composed by man. Beethoven spoke to me so personally, so intimately, I felt as if he had written the music just for me. His music, though complex, was approachable, simple and, at the same time, powerful.

I also found myself excited by the performances of Yehudi Menuhin, Béla Bartók, Isaac Stern and Gregor Piatigorsky. When George Enescu (known in France as Georges Enesco) conducted his *Romanian Rhapsody* at the Trocadéro, I was there. Music filled me with joy and excitement, and I often lulled myself to sleep humming excerpts of the music I had heard earlier in the evening. It made me feel whole and strong.

During this period of my life, I had a vision of Stefa being near me. She was as beautiful as ever and winking at me again, full of smiles and softness. The sweetness of her image, mixed with the pain of losing her, convinced me I'd been profoundly foolish to leave her. One night, unable to sleep for thinking of her, I rose in the wee hours and wrote her a long letter, in which I described my new life in Paris – my musical adventures, my love of the sights. I told her how much I missed her and expressed my love for her. I also asked whether she might join me in Paris and suggested the two of us might travel to the States together. The hope of reuniting with Stefa brought feelings of joyful anticipation, albeit cautious anticipation.

A letter from Luba reached me in February, informing me that she, Moniek and Nathan were about to leave for Uruguay.

A day later, a letter arrived from Stefa. My heart skipped a beat. I tore open the envelope to find a photograph of Stefa, posing in her nurse's uniform and beaming with happiness. She'd written a few warm words of greeting on the back. The letter, by contrast, was full of detail about her daily routine and present life in the camp. She was still waiting for a visa to the United States, she said, but also mentioned that she might be travelling to Palestine with a friend. She thanked me for writing to her and remembering her, and stated that she was still fond of me and wished me good luck in the States.

I was hurt and disappointed, of course, but had no one to blame but myself.

I decided to take a long weekend to visit Luba and her family before their departure to South America. At the same time, I carried the secret, sweet hope that I might be able to see Stefa while in Landsberg and convince her to come with me to Paris.

I surprised Luba, who was thrilled to see me. I told her about my life in Paris and spoke to her as if she were my younger sister. The tables had turned, it seemed. She and Moniek were still living on handouts, while I was gainfully employed and thriving as a Parisian. I had become worldlier, full of energy and hope.

Luba handed Nathan to me. I tickled his cheek, and he smiled sweetly.

She then told me that their plans had changed, that they would be going to Uruguay a month or two later and might even stop in Paris to see me on the way.

A little while later, Moniek arrived home from his Saturday evening prayers. He greeted me with restraint, his gaze betraying a bit of reproach for my having travelled on the Sabbath.

In the morning, I said goodbye to my only sibling, with whom I had spent the worst of times, as well as the best, during the catastrophic war.

I then hurried across the camp to Stefa's room in the barrack. I held my breath as I knocked on her door.

When it opened a moment later, there she stood, eyes wide with amazement.

I shook her hand, but it was limp. And when I attempted to draw her close, she did not respond.

'Come in and have some coffee,' she said finally.

We sat down, and I told her of my good fortune, including my hope to leave soon for the United States.

'Yes, I remember,' she replied, telling me that she'd read my letter.

'I wanted to thank you for the lovely letter you sent, and the beautiful photo,' I said. 'I was anxiously waiting to hear from you.'

She had not written back right away, she explained, because she was dating another man. She hoped to go to Palestine with him, since she had grown tired of waiting for a visa to the States.

'In a few years,' I said, 'I'll be a citizen of the United States, and I could bring you over.'

'A few years is a *long* time…'

I was silent for a moment, then turned to her boldly. 'Stefa, I want to marry you. Then I'm sure I'll find a way for us to go to America together.'

She hesitated. Then, in a resolute voice, she said, 'I want to go to Palestine. Arik and I want our children to live in their own country.' Her determined jaw line and trembling lips conveyed the words she could not say: She was pregnant.

Her silent revelation was a knife to the heart, leaving me speechless. I stood, embraced her gently and said goodbye.

Stefa's image remained with me all the way back to Paris, and long thereafter.

***

In late March I met Joseph Gitman in the arrondissement's cafeteria, a natural gathering place for Jewish refugees and transients. I was pleased to see him, and he seemed of similar cheer. He was on his way to the States, he said, and, like me, would be residing in Paris for six months to establish his residency. He had arrived a few days earlier and had found a room in another dilapidated hotel not far from my hovel.

While we ate, I couldn't stop talking about my Hillel scholarship and my adventures in Paris. We had shifted roles. I knew far more French and knew much more about the city. I felt at home here, while he was the stranger, bewildered by the awesomeness of it all.

For the next few weeks, I saw little of Joseph. He, too, had enrolled at the Alliance Française and had almost no spare time.

Passover that year fell in mid-April, and the seder was conducted in the cafeteria by a young rabbi who spoke French. It sounded strange to me, although I had become comfortable with the language and knew most of the melodies and sang them with gusto. The Joint provided the kosher meal.

The next morning, Joseph and I visited the famed Rothschild synagogue near the Place de la Concorde. As we entered, we fetched prayer shawls and prayer books and joined in the services. Although it should not have surprised me, the prayers were essentially the same as those in the prayer books of Dubno, as were the melodies of the important ones. The cantor, a well-trained tenor, and the male choir sang the *Prayer for Dew*, composed by Yossele Rosenblatt, which I knew well. The prayer was so moving that I felt as if transported to the Great Synagogue of Dubno, where I had sung as a soprano in Cantor Sherman's choir. I had not been to a synagogue, nor heard a cantor and choir, since leaving home nearly six years before. It was as though a part of me had returned home after a long absence.

After leaving the synagogue, we stopped for lunch at the cafeteria, where I shared with Joseph my elation at being part of the service and listening to classic cantorial music. 'But to whom are we praying?' I asked.

Joseph reminded me that I had posed the same question a year ago, after we had visited the synagogue in Dubno. 'I thought my answer at the time impressed you, no?'

'I liked your explanation that God is an ideal of perfection to which we should aspire. But our prayers address a specific divine presence, sometimes with human features.'

Joseph reminded me that, in his view, the prayers were composed by gifted poets eager to clothe the idea of God with beautiful, creative words and thoughts, but that God does not really need our prayers and that we cannot even know if He exists. 'God does not *need* us. We need *Him*. We need an ideal to give us hope in times of distress, to empower us when our own strength fails. This ideal gives us a mooring, a spiritual anchor.'

Joseph's words had a profound effect on me. I gained enormous respect for him.

It was the first time in my life that I began to see my Jewish religion, sketched out by Joseph, as a meaningful way of understanding the world around me and my relationship to that world – without clutter, torturous interpretations, or imagery. I felt comfortable with these ideas and gained a renewed pride in being a Jew.

***

In May 1947 Luba, Moniek and their infant son, Nathan, did indeed come to Paris, having finally obtained their visas to Uruguay. They had arranged, with the help of the Joint, to stop for a week in the city to visit me. The Joint even located a hotel room for them.

Six months had passed since I had seen them last. My sister, brother-in-law and their baby had changed so much. Luba's face harboured more wrinkles, and I noted a fair bit of grey in her hair. Moniek, too, had aged noticeably during the short period. There was something deeply sad and severe about the look of them, and I guessed they'd been through hell waiting for their visas to come through.

Luba now covered her head with a kerchief, and she wore a long dress with long sleeves, just as the ultra-Orthodox women in the camp did. I asked her what Moniek was going to do in Uruguay.

'God knows,' she said, and went on to extol Moniek's knack for invention. 'He's brimming with all sorts of ideas.' She gave a small smile. 'God will help.'

'And what are you going to do?'

'Maybe I'll find a job as a teacher, God willing.'

Most of her sentences, I noted, included the phrases 'God willing' or 'God will help.'

What was done was done, but, even so, Luba's transformation made me uneasy. Our home in Dubno had been traditional, but far removed from ultra-Orthodoxy. Mom held liberal views of religion and Judaism, whereas Luba had played the rebel, professing disbelief in a personal God, much to the chagrin of our parents. During our travels and sojourn in the Soviet Union, Luba and I had practised little Judaism. We had been children of Jewish heritage but not truly Jewish in practice.

A year and a half of marriage to Moniek had changed Luba into a person I hardly recognized. Moniek, too, had become stricter in his observance of Jewish laws and mores and still occasionally taunted me for being a non-believer. To my deep dismay, I found myself uncomfortable around my own sister and brother-in-law, and I resented that religion had begun to pry us apart.

In a private moment with Luba, I relayed my concern about the growing gulf between us.

'One day you'll be married,' she countered with reproach, 'and you'll see what it takes to share a life with somebody. Moniek is a good man, and he needs his way of practising religion to feel wholesome, to feel happy. Am I to deny him this happiness?' She relaxed some and took my hand. 'I'll be all right. Don't worry.'

Maybe she makes sense, I thought. But Moniek's increasingly autocratic ways still troubled me. His determination to control and direct daily tasks, along with his quick temper toward Luba if she dared to contradict him in any way, were not, in my mind, the traits of a good and loving husband. Had religion, I wondered, become an excuse for him to be overbearing?

I spent time with Luba and Moniek daily, after work, but I came to be more guarded in expressing my thoughts. A palpable tension crept into our relationship. Nonetheless, I shared in Luba and Moniek's happiness together and their hopes for the future.

Our aunt and uncle in Uruguay had written to Luba and Moniek, stating that they would be living in their own apartment and that Luba would be able to find work as a teacher in the Hebrew school. Moniek, too, would have no difficulty obtaining work. By this time, he had perfected the electric shaver and hoped to market it in Uruguay. He shared with me several other ingenious ideas with the same excitement as when I first met him. Both seemed determined to do well, and I knew they had the talent and tenacity to do so.

I took Luba, Moniek and little Nathan for long walks through the streets of Paris. One late afternoon we went up the Eiffel Tower and admired the city below, stretched before us as a huge panorama of parks, monuments, and wide streets. I delighted in being able to shepherd my beloved visitors around the city as if a native Parisian.

Two days later, I accompanied Luba and Moniek to Saint Lazare Station, where they would take the train to Spain, and then board a ship to Uruguay. I held little Nathan on my shoulders while Luba and Moniek carried their belongings. The thought of our separation pained me, leaving me silently distraught as I cheered them on. 'In a few years, I will be a citizen of the United States,' I said, 'and I will be able to bring you to America if things don't work out in Uruguay.' It was as much wishful thinking as reassurance – to me and to them.

I boarded the train, helped them get settled, and bade them goodbye.

As I turned to leave, Luba ran after me, pulled me toward her, and held me for a long time, her cheeks streaked with tears. 'Take good care of yourself, my brother.'

'Please write to me, *Lubushka Golubushka*', I said, using one of my old terms of endearment for her. 'You are the only one I have left in the world.'

As I hopped down to the platform, my thoughts swept back to six years earlier, in Shepetovka, where Luba and I learned how to jump onto a moving train.

There would be no more running for trains, expecting a bullet in the back. We had indeed come a long way. The war was over, and we were still alive. Luba and Moniek seemed secure, and I, before long, would travel to the States to pursue my dreams.

The locomotive's whistle blew, and the train pulled away. I waved goodbye to Luba and Moniek, who were glued to the window of their car. The world of my youth had been destroyed. They were all I had left.

Watching them go firmly closed the door on my past. I felt utterly alone.

After their train was out of sight, I left the station and walked toward the River Seine. It was a beautiful Sunday afternoon with the sun reflecting off the river like so many mirrors dancing on the waves. People strolled along the promenade, passing vendors and jesters, as doves cooed from little alcoves. I spied two lovers sitting on a bench, locked in a passionate embrace. The image transported me back to that Sunday a year earlier, lying beside Stefa – how she had been the one to take the initiative. And her words to me in the hospital, months earlier: 'Live a little, Meesha.'

I felt the blood pulsating in my veins and quickened my step. It was time to start a new life, I decided.

And I did not walk alone. Hope walked silently beside me.

✳✳✳

Bastille Day, 14 July

Colourful crowds, military parades, jesters, and vendors filled the streets, stirring much excitement and camaraderie. People danced, embraced one another, and sang harmoniously in unison, as if led by an invisible

Painful Parting

© Copyright February 2008, Don Bloom, E. Brunswick, NJ.

conductor. The *Marseillaise* blared from every loudspeaker. The motto of the French Revolution – *Liberté, égalité, fraternité* – proved alive and well. In the evening, I shared my enthusiasm with Joseph, telling him how the motto – liberty, equality, brotherhood – impressed me.

'They don't tell much of the bloodshed that went on,' he said. 'Of the thousands of innocent people butchered by the guillotine, the hatred the revolution generated between kin and friends, the cauldron of violence it ignited, the rise of Napoleon and the deaths of hundreds of thousands during the Napoleonic Wars that followed it all.'

Joseph had a point. The French Revolution had brought respectability to violence, even to random violence, just as the Russian Revolution had done, giving rise to slave-labour camps and the wanton killing of innocents that, in turn, paved the way for the Holocaust, had it not?

Joseph came back heatedly to expound his belief that all of Western culture, particularly since the French Revolution, had lost its moral footing.

***

When I returned to my apartment after leaving Joseph, the concierge handed me a thin envelope addressed with familiar handwriting. It was from Stefa! A short note inside informed me that she and her friend Arik were set to leave Landsberg by bus for Italy, and then depart for Palestine. She hoped to soon be in the land of her dreams. She wished me a good life in America and good luck finding a woman I could love – somewhat caustically, I thought.

In an offhand manner, she told me of a young Soviet exchange-student nurse at St. Ottilien Hospital. She was a beautiful Uzbek woman, Stefa wrote, and had inquired about Meesha Kesler.

Mahdu.

Stefa asked if I had known such a woman, but said she stopped short of disclosing my whereabouts.

Her note touched me profoundly, as did my regrets.

I hurt them both, I thought remorsefully.

More than that, I could have had a wonderful life with Stefa. Or, maybe I should have stayed in Samarkand with Mahdu and spared myself the excruciating pain of seeing the mass grave in Dubno. Also, the shame of being an unwanted Jew in Germany.

A quiet thought entered my mind. *Did Mahdu travel all the way to Germany because of me?* What a wonderful, determined woman she was. I wondered, wistfully, if I'd ever be able to tell her that in person.

***

Late in July news that the British navy had intercepted a ship heading from France to Palestine pervaded the airwaves and the press. The *Exodus 1947* carried more than 4,500 Jewish refugees who had languished in DP camps in Germany. They did not have permission from the British to land in Palestine, however. I followed with ire the unfolding drama of the passengers' resistance to the British navy, which resulted in several fatalities.

Subsequently, the navy forcibly returned the refugees to Germany. I wondered whether the passengers included any of my friends from Landsberg, alarmed by the thought that Stefa and her boyfriend might be among those who were turned back, or worse.

More than ever, I was anxious to leave this war-torn, blood-soaked continent. And in early August I finally obtained my papers to travel to the United States.

A day later, full of excitement and anticipation, I visited the radio shop and bade goodbye to François. I saw Joseph, too, who told me that he expected to leave for America in a month or so and expressed his hope that we would soon see each other again. I then fetched my few belongings and boarded the train for Le Havre, where I took a ferry to Southampton.

In England, I boarded the *Marine Fletcher* to cross the Atlantic. The small ship had been used to transport military personnel. The first evening, we were welcomed with a reception of overwhelming variety – and quantity – of foods, the likes of which I'd never seen. I ate with wild abandon. Alas, this was my first and last big meal on the voyage, due to becoming violently seasick.

Seven days later, I was relieved to see the Statue of Liberty beckoning me to the land of promise. I disembarked at a Hudson pier on 17 August 1947.

Manhattan stunned me with its might and splendour. In the subsequent two weeks, as I walked its streets overshadowed by skyscrapers, I felt like a Lilliputian in *Gulliver's Travels* – small and insignificant. But I also felt pumped up. There was so much to see and do, especially for an engineer.

The Hebrew Immigrant Aid Society (HIAS), which had taken over my care in those early weeks, placed me with a family from my hometown that had come to the United States in the 1930s. My short stay with them helped to quiet my nerves and soften the shock of the new language and culture. I covered long distances on foot and traveled by subway and bus to familiarize myself with all of the city's boroughs. I also tried to squeeze in as much vocabulary as I could with the help of my worn-out English-French dictionary.

A few days before departing for Maine, I went, courtesy of HIAS, to meet my benefactors at Hillel headquarters in Washington, DC. Marie Syrkin, who had helped to arrange my scholarship, greeted me. She introduced me to Hillel's head, Dr. Abram Sachar, a historian who subsequently founded Brandeis University in Massachusetts. I learned that the efforts of Dr. Sachar, Ms. Syrkin and their associates had placed more than sixty DP students in various US universities – sight unseen – myself among them. The scholarship they described, which would pay for four years' tuition plus living expenses, left me in awe.

On 1 September 1947, I arrived in Waterville, Maine. Colby College was on the move at that time to its new campus on Mayflower Hill. Mrs. Frieda Lubell, of the B'nai B'rith Women's Auxiliary, her husband Moe, and their two young children hosted me for the next two weeks, and I became a member of their family for many years to come.

After my stay with the Lubell family, I moved into the new dorms at Colby College. The smell of fresh paint taunted my nostrils and my mind. I felt alive and elated, as if airborne. The nightmare of the past six years receded. Gone was the lawless jungle of violence and cruelty. No more need to run and hide. There was nothing to fear! A magic curtain lifted the worry and despair, opening before me a kaleidoscope of possibility, hope, and promise.

Colby, a fine liberal arts college, maintained a relaxed, almost fairy-tale-like academic environment. The first few months challenged me, however, as I worked to master the English language – particularly the colloquial form spoken by my classmates.

Late in the first semester, around Christmastime, I experienced my first major language-related blunder. I had taken a liking to an attractive classmate, Alice Moskowitz, who had travelled home to Mount Vernon, New York, for winter vacation. She had left her address with me, and after receiving a charming note from her, I wrote her back a lengthy letter, concluding with, 'Come soon. I *expect* to see you.'

My letter went unanswered.

When I approached her on campus after the holiday, she was openly critical. 'You wrote to me as if you owned me,' she snapped. 'You have no right to *expect* anything from me.' When I explained what I had intended to say, she countered, 'You should have said, I'm *hoping* to see you.'

It took a lot more studying to master the subtleties and nuances of the language to avoid further missteps.

My freshman year at Colby was a tonic and a blessing, covering English, the humanities, and the basic sciences. In second semester, I took on several more science courses and performed well – so much so that my physics professor suggested I transfer to the Massachusetts Institute of Technology, his alma mater. He helped me fill out an application and even wrote me a letter of recommendation.

Two weeks later, a letter from MIT was waiting for me when I got home from classes. I'd been accepted! It was hard, almost impossible, to believe that soon I would be a second-year engineering student at MIT.

The last few weeks at Colby set me in turmoil. The thought of entering such a venerable institution gave me joy, but also trepidation.

Am I ready for this?

To date, I'd had a piecemeal, erratic education, particularly in the sciences. I knew that MIT students came from the upper levels of American society, whereas I had come from a simple, modest home in the small town of Dubno, Poland. Would I fit in socially among better-educated, more sophisticated students?

Adrift again, far away from my roots, I wistfully imagined my parents and how happy they would be, seeing their son studying to be an engineer in such a lofty place.

Would they even recognize me?

I wished I could talk to Luba, but she was so far away.

At the end of second semester, I left the laid-back atmosphere of Colby, soon to plunge into one of the most competitive engineering schools in the country. My burning wings had carried me to dizzying heights, indeed. I had triumphed.

Commentary I

The Yalta Conference

Preamble

With the military situation rapidly changing, the three leaders of the alliance felt it imperative to meet face-to-face to review the war's end-game strategy as well as emerging postwar issues. At Stalin's urging, the leaders would meet at the abandoned resort palaces of Russian tsars on the Crimean Peninsula in the Black Sea. There, the three leaders and their entourages, numbering well over a thousand, were to decide the fate of the millions of war-tossed peoples of Europe.

The leaders had a common goal: to map out a strategy for quickly concluding the war and to effect a smooth transition of power in the countries they were about to occupy. But each leader's vision of how to achieve these goals varied, based on his national and political interests, as well as his background and ethos. In brief, Stalin wanted to assure possession of the countries that his army would occupy and to expand his sphere of influence. FDR and Churchill aimed to moderate Stalin's goals.

The Preamble presents portraits of the three leaders and their reflections about one other, as well as the important issues they would face in dealing with each other. I formulated this material long after the war, based on accounts in the Soviet press, new research, and personal memories of many of the events stretching back three-quarters of a century.

I have labelled the three Allied leaders – Stalin, Roosevelt, and Churchill – the Super-Egotist, the Idealist, and the Realist.

***

In a 1 July 1941 radio address to his country, Stalin proclaimed: 'Future historians will state that Hitler started the war, but Stalin finished it.' Indeed, Stalin proved this and then some. He had transformed a nearly defeated Red Army into the mightiest in the world. He had expanded Soviet boundaries and secured a huge and uncontested sphere of influence. The recent successes of his brilliant generals opened the gates to all of Europe, which lay devastated and begging for rescue and order. His Communist allies were all too eager to swoop in and take the reins of government in most of those countries. In fact, nearly all the Eurasian continent was in turmoil. Stalin dominated the continent as no one before him. Vast stretches of it lay ready for his grab.

Stalin's own country, however, had suffered enormous losses.[1] In order to rebuild it, he desperately needed capital and resources. The United States had a seemingly inexhaustible supply of both, of which Roosevelt appeared to be in firm control. Stalin made a decision to draw closer to Roosevelt.

Stalin was eager to meet with the two leaders, both of whom he had met previously in Tehran in the fall of 1943, where they had professed friendship toward the Soviet Union. But why had they delayed the opening of the Western Front for nearly two years while his people were shedding blood, fighting the brutal enemy alone? Why had it taken Eisenhower's forces more than half a year to move only a few hundred kilometers into territory hostile to the Germans? Stalin's generals viewed with contempt the cautious, tentative attacks of the US and British forces near Belgium, where they were nearly surrounded by the Germans. He would soon have the opportunity to test the sincerity of their declared friendship.

One thing he saw clearly: He wanted to see their Expeditionary Force finish its limited role and leave Europe as soon as possible. Ergo, he would be patient with and cordial to his guests, particularly Roosevelt.

Stalin did not cherish the prospect of listening to Churchill's long-winded oratory. He preferred his own crisp pronouncements to drive home his points more forcefully and clearly.

Churchill liked to extol his own bravery in saving Europe from Hitler. The facts, however, were quite different. If Churchill and his buddies had listened to Stalin, the war could have been avoided altogether. By August 1939, Hitler had already swallowed up Austria, the Sudetenland, and half of Czechoslovakia. He then confronted the British and French with endless unspecified demands for more territory. England and France lacked both the stomach for all-out warfare and the military power to fight Hitler. Stalin offered to move his mighty forces to the Polish-German border to confront Hitler. He wanted France and Great Britain – unprepared as they were – to mobilize their forces and stop Hitler in the West while his Red Army attacked the Germans in the East. Doing that surely would have dissuaded Hitler from further aggression.

Yet Poland, shielded by the Polish-British Common Defense Pact signed just a month earlier, refused to permit Soviet forces to enter her territory, and Churchill and his cronies did nothing to convince the Poles to withdraw their objections. Stalin proved the stupidity of Churchill and his ilk by extending a hand of friendship to Hitler, giving rise to the Molotov-Ribbentrop Pact that gave Hitler the green light to attack Poland. He remembered the episode well, even though Churchill and his colleagues in the West may have forgotten. Indeed, wasn't it Churchill, or one of his friends in the House of Commons, who had uttered the phrase 'a plague on both your houses', referring to Hitler and Stalin, confessing their ill will toward him?

Besides, Churchill had little to offer, either for concluding the war or reconstructing the continent. He led his country, with much fanfare, to fight Hitler but with insufficient means to do so. In the process, he impoverished Great Britain and shook to the core the entire British Empire, which would surely collapse under its own weight before long. Great Britain might consider itself to be a lion, but its roar had been stifled and would be further weakened in the postwar jungle.

Roosevelt, on the other hand, impressed Stalin with his competence and leadership qualities. He admired Roosevelt's ability to conduct war on the three continents of Africa, Europe, and Asia, across the vastness of the Pacific. He appreciated Roosevelt's ability to introduce socialist practices that helped to rescue the United States and much of Europe from the grip of the Great Depression. Was he replicating Stalin's economic reforms, which had saved the Soviet Union? The Soviet Union, under his leadership, had achieved the greatest military might on earth. The United States, under Roosevelt, constituted the globe's greatest economic power. A good rapport between the two would offer splendid opportunities for rebuilding and uniting the world under the banner of socialism, he mused.

Roosevelt had indicated a need to befriend Stalin – an offer Stalin would readily accept with opened arms. Personally, he liked Roosevelt's good humour and ease with people. Yet, Stalin had heard reports about the US president's failing health and worried about who would succeed him if he died.

Roosevelt came to the conference confident that he could befriend Stalin and mollify his demands. He believed he could turn Stalin into a true ally – one who would work closely with the United States for a just, lasting peace in Europe and beyond. He based this faith on his success of winning four consecutive four-year terms as president of a country beset by overwhelming difficulties at home and abroad. His mettle had been tested over and over during endless hours of negotiation with domestic rivals and numerous foreign leaders, including those whose policies ran contrary to US interests. He had honed his fireside chats well enough that over sixty million listeners tuned in eagerly week after week.

On his long voyage by sea to the Yalta Conference, the president had much information and many thoughts to digest. Eisenhower's army had won the Battle of the Bulge, the last great push of the German army in the West. He also relished the thought that the victory at Albans had opened for the United States the road to the very heart of the enemy, the industrial Ruhr, and, beyond that, Berlin. The defeated German generals were secretly begging to make peace with America. No, he would have none of that. He'd rather work with US allies to complete the job.

The war's toll on America, although not unendurable, proved heavier than Roosevelt had anticipated. Overall US casualties, approaching four hundred thousand, amounted to a small fraction of those suffered by the Japanese or the Germans, and particularly by the Soviet Union, whose military casualties reportedly exceeded seven million. His declaration at his first inaugural address, that the nation had 'nothing to fear but fear itself', had served him well through the years of the Great Depression and in the past three years of war.

And yet, elements of fear began to occupy the president's mind.

The Red Army's rapid advance westward against enormous enemy resistance, although on one hand reassuring, concerned him. What if Stalin decided to move his forces beyond the tentative borders agreed upon in Tehran all the way to the English Channel? He knew well that Eisenhower's Expeditionary Force couldn't match the formidable Soviets, tested in the battles of Moscow, Stalingrad, and Smolensk. He was warily conscious of rising sympathy for Communism in devastated Europe and the Soviets' increasing ability to undermine existing, weak governments in favour of ones sympathetic to the Soviet Union. In fact, Stalin's moves in the months preceding the conference gave him much concern. The Red Army's conquests paved the way for commissars to turn the occupied countries into Soviet satellites. Fearing repression by the new regimes, millions of people fled in panic, causing havoc and human suffering.

Roosevelt was uncomfortable with the concept of dividing Europe into 'spheres of influence', a concept Stalin had injected into the proceedings of the Tehran Conference. An idealist in foreign affairs in the mould of Woodrow Wilson, Roosevelt wanted each liberated country to become democratic and independent. He envisioned a peaceful evolution of the countries into a unified Europe. These were the concepts that he and Churchill had worked out and drafted under the Atlantic Charter.[2]

A more profound, personal concern also churned in Roosevelt's mind: Should he trust Stalin? Stalin had plenty of blood on his hands, with several million Ukrainian farmers having been uprooted from their homes and farms and scattered throughout the land, including Siberia, which led to the deaths of most. Roosevelt had even read of Stalin having his own wife murdered.

His personal physician, as well as his daughter, Anna, fretted over Roosevelt's weakening 'ticker,' but his state of mind and his power to think buoyed his spirits. He looked forward to an exciting week of meetings and negotiations.

A plethora of challenges faced Winston Churchill. Nearly five years earlier, he had entered the House of Commons as the country's new leader and proclaimed: 'I have nothing to offer but blood, toil, tears, and sweat.' That fiery call to arms rallied his people to stand by him during some of Great Britain's darkest hours. He defended Britain's existence, but at unbearable cost, weakening the empire's economic foundation. His people lost patience. They wanted bread, not more war. The colonies, particularly India, seethed with discontent, giving rise to widespread violence. The man in the loincloth, Mahatma Gandhi, had visited Churchill at 10 Downing Street, promising to hold his fire so as not to embarrass Britain during the war. But Churchill suspected that Gandhi was readying to stage another hunger strike in an effort to incite the Indian subcontinent to force Britain out. Impoverished by the war, Great Britain had insufficient means to bring peace to the restless countries of its empire. Thus, Churchill became anxious to end the war in Europe. And Stalin would be indispensable in achieving that goal.

He worried, however, about putting too much trust in Stalin.

The case of the mysterious disappearance of some twenty-six thousand Polish prisoners justified Churchill's concerns about the Soviet leader. Churchill had helped draft the British-Polish agreement for mutual self-defense. At Stalin's urging, Great Britain had entered the war two days after Hitler invaded Poland. Two weeks after the invasion, Stalin's forces moved to occupy the eastern half of Poland. A few months later, Stalin's secret police corralled fifteen thousand Polish officers and some eleven thousand Polish intelligentsia and communal leaders and deported them to the woods of Katyn. Churchill was unable to get a credible answer from Soviet authorities, even those at the highest level, to his inquiries regarding the fate of these people. According to documents supplied to Churchill by the Polish government-in-exile in London, Stalin's secret police had shot and buried them in mass graves.

But Churchill was a realist. He scoffed at Roosevelt's idealist notion that he could change the stripes of Stalin's tiger-like instincts. Churchill felt that Roosevelt, to whom he professed deep friendship and even love, did not fully comprehend the workings of the megalomaniacal dictator. Churchill had an innate hostility toward dictators, and he considered Stalin's savagery a mere grade below that of Hitler. Still, Stalin had become an essential ally and one who had done more than his share to bring Hitler close to defeat.

The ongoing election in Great Britain confounded and irritated Churchill no end. He trusted the democratic process of free elections. But his earlier presumption, that the British would reward his heroic efforts in saving the country and reelect him, seemed to be fading. Clement Attlee, head of the British Labour Party, appeared to be gaining on him. (Churchill held little respect for Attlee and was said to have quipped words to the effect that Attlee was a modest man and rightly so.)

Above all else, Churchill had good reason to worry about Roosevelt's well-being and his stamina to withstand the rigours of negotiation. Would he, Churchill, feeling more like Shakespeare's ageing King Lear than the leader of a mighty nation, be able to defend effectively the interests of the West? He had a queasy intuition that Stalin and Roosevelt would sideline him at the conference.

***

Roosevelt arrived in visibly poor health, which deteriorated further as the conference went on. His participation was limited to a few hours per day. Stalin, although the same age as Roosevelt, showed much more vigour and energy, and soon dominated the agenda and the main articles of the agreements to be signed by the leaders. He proved a masterful debater, wearing down his opponents with patience and logic.

***

The Conference

Conference Agenda

The plenary sessions kept the staff busy day and night, recording and interpreting the proceedings. Vyacheslav Molotov, Stalin's right-hand man and foreign minister, supported by his staff, sat in charge of the exact wording of the Articles of Agreement. Edward Stettinius Jr., US secretary of state, who had limited knowledge of foreign affairs, proved to be no match for the experienced and well-prepared Molotov.

Poland's fate was of especial interest to me. Drawing up that nation's new boundaries was high on the conference agenda, and one of its more controversial issues as well. Stalin presented his firm position that the Soviet Union could not tolerate Poland becoming a hostile conduit for would-be Soviet enemies. His view prevailed. The eastern part of Poland captured by the Soviets in 1939, including my hometown, would again revert to the Soviet Union. An equivalent eastern portion of Germany would be transferred to Poland. The agreement acknowledged that moving the Polish boundaries westward into Germany would involve extensive relocation of people.

This prospect didn't sit well with Roosevelt, but he acceded to it.

More difficulties arose when trying to determine which entity would govern the liberated Poland. The Polish government-in-exile, which had actively participated in the war, anticipated re-taking the reins of its country, while Molotov considered the Communist-leaning provisional government, which he had installed a year earlier, to be the legitimate one.

Similar difficulties plagued the conference on issues related to defining the legitimacy of other governments in the liberated territories. Molotov introduced language that subtly defined democratic governments as those friendly to the Soviet Union and any other as fascist. Those nuances would legitimize the Soviet Union's imposition of governments of its choice for countries occupied by the Red Army.

***

Deliberations while planning the Allied forces' movements in the waning months of the war created other misunderstandings. Stalin promised Roosevelt that his forces would not rush to occupy Berlin, which Roosevelt interpreted to mean that Eisenhower's Expeditionary Force, which had suffered great losses in the Battle of the Bulge, need not move too rapidly eastward, thereby minimizing further casualties. Despite this supposed understanding, Stalin ordered Marshal Zhukov, in charge of the Red Army in the south and centre, to move toward Berlin at full speed. As a result, the Soviets succeeded in being the first to enter and occupy the city.

During the following four months, the Red Army sustained losses of four hundred thousand, approximating the total US Army casualties of the Second World War. That heavy price, however, achieved Stalin's goal of dominating the part of Europe that included Berlin and everything to its east.

Descriptions of the proceedings conveyed a heated discussion on German reparations, with Stalin adopting a punitive stance and Roosevelt and Churchill inclined to be more conciliatory, due to fears of repeating the mistake of imposing huge reparations on Germany. The debate ended in a compromise of ten billion dollars in reparations to the Soviet Union, payable with equivalent transportable industrial assets. Once again, Stalin's iron will prevailed.

Notes

1. Selected items of Soviet war losses:

   Human casualties – 26 million.
   Population down by 14%.
   Destruction included more than 1,700 towns, 70,000 villages, 40,000 miles RR track, 100,000 collective farms.
   Overall national wealth down by one third.
   Harvests had been cut in half.
   Tractor production down by 76%.
   Steel production down by 33%.
   Oil production down by 38% (see Reference 6)

2. The so-called Atlantic Charter included eight 'common principles' that the United States and Great Britain would be committed to supporting in the world. Both countries agreed not to seek territorial expansion; to seek the liberalization of international trade; to establish freedom of the seas; and to support international labour, economic, and welfare standards. Most importantly, both the United States and Great Britain were committed to supporting the restoration of self-governments for all countries that had been occupied during the war and allowing all peoples to choose their own form of government (see Reference 49).

Commentary II

The Concentration/Death Camps and Death Marches

The concentration camps contained industrial and manufacturing facilities, often run by major German corporations that used the inmates as slave labourers. Inmates were put to heavy work while subsisting on starvation rations until, exhausted, they were sent to the gas chambers.

Ilya Ehrenburg became my main source of information on German atrocities in Belarus and Ukraine, which the Germans occupied from 1941 through the spring of 1944. Emerging as the most important columnist of *Izvestia*, Ehrenburg wrote often of Jewish persecution in Europe before and, in particular, during the war. Other correspondents soon came forward to shed light on the bestial behaviour of the Germans.

Ehrenburg devoted most of his remaining years to documenting, with copious interviews of surviving Jews, the grisly story of the Holocaust in the Soviet Union, resulting in the definitive book *The Complete Black Book of Russian Jewry*, co-authored by Vasily Grossman (Ref. 7). More recently, Joshua Rubinstein and Ilya Altman authored a related book, *The Unknown Black Book*, based on documents on the Holocaust in the Soviet Union made available after the beginning of glasnost in 1986 (Ref. 36).

What I had learned from the Soviet press was but a prelude to the data painstakingly accumulated in the following years and decades. In sum, the Germans had built as many as fourteen thousand concentration/death camps, a number that includes camps that served as satellites to the several hundred main killing centres (Ref. 42). The Commentary will focus on the main concentration/death camps of Poland.

The exposed atrocities of the concentration and death camps stunned the Western world, and particularly Jews who had lived through the war. Gathering evidence of the barbarity of a nation at the centre of Western civilization proved a deeply painful and traumatic experience for survivors, as well as for the many chroniclers of the catastrophe. It would take years for the gruesome personal accounts, related facts and statistics to emerge.

My own heart-rending visit to the mass grave on the outskirts of Dubno, where lay my parents and relatives, continued to haunt me, prompting a paralyzing fear of speaking, hearing, or, particularly, reading about the cataclysm that had befallen my people. The Nuremberg trials of the Nazi hierarchy in the fall of 1945 awakened me to the enormity of the crimes the Germans had committed, particularly against the Jews. Their cold-blooded testimonies, speciously justifying their behaviour, stunned me.

The capture of Adolf Eichmann in Argentina, and his trial in Jerusalem in 1961, added to my growing desire to learn more. Eichmann's admissions of the unspeakable crimes he committed – and dared justify, by quoting Kant and the importance of duty and obedience – infuriated me. He exhibited no trace of guilt or shame for having commandeered and organized the extermination of more than four hundred thousand Hungarian Jews near the end of the war. His testimony, when added to those of the principal Nazi leaders, undermined the very foundation of Western culture, which had served as my cultural cradle. I felt suddenly bereft, not only of my home, parents, and relatives, but of having any solid foundation as a humane human being. I was further incensed that the entire Western world, including the United States, had been aware of the mass killings of Jews but had done little to stop it.

The Polish Concentration/Death Camps and Death Marches

In 1944, the Red Army, moving rapidly westward, continued to uncover and report on the major concentration and death camps in Poland: Treblinka, Auschwitz-Birkenau, Plaszow, Chelmno, Majdanek, Sobibor, Belzec and Trostenets. Notably, these camps were near major cities, populated in large measure by Jews, sometimes over 50 per cent: Warsaw, Krakow, Lodz, Lublin, Vilna, Lvov and Minsk. Thus, Treblinka II had been established in 1942 exclusively to exterminate Jews from Warsaw and its vicinity, meaning nearly all of its nine hundred thousand victims were Jewish. Approximately one million Jews perished in Auschwitz of a total of 1.1 million victims, etc. (Ref. 42). The main Polish camps exterminated approximately 2.7 million (Ref. 47) of the six million Jewish victims of the Holocaust. More than three million Jewish victims perished by bullet or by asphyxiation in gas vans in Ukraine and Belarus (Ref. 4, Ref. 36). The rate of extermination in these camps – set up for industrialized mass-murder – approximated three thousand people per day during their nearly three years of operation.

Toward the end of the war, in a frenzied effort to cover up their crimes, the Germans exhumed the mass graves in the death and concentration camps and burned the unearthed corpses.

On 12 April 1945, General Patton, accompanying General Eisenhower, inspected the Ohrdruf concentration camp, part of the Buchenwald network of camps. The following is an excerpt from his report of that visit:

> When we began to approach with our troops, the Germans thought it expedient to remove the evidence of their crime…they had some of the slaves exhume the bodies and place them on a mammoth griddle composed of 60-centimetre railway tracks laid on brick foundations. They poured pitch on the bodies and then built a fire of pinewood and coal under them. (Ref. 48)

The Germans feared even more the repercussions of leaving behind inmates who could bear witness against them and so decided to transport the barely alive prisoners by train, westward toward Germany's centre.

With fewer trains becoming available, the Germans resorted to marching the starving inmates to several camps in Germany, with Bergen-Belsen bearing the brunt of the exhausted masses.

Hundreds of thousands of those forced to march west perished en route.

Author Dan Stone (Ref. 42) states that in January 1945, the death and concentration camps contained a total of 714,000 inmates; that number decreased to 400,000 by the end of the war. It can be assumed that the majority of those who perished between January and May of 1945 were death-marchers. A good portion of the more than 300,000 death marchers who perished were Jewish, since many of these marches originated in the largely Jewish death and concentration camps of Poland. Isabella Leitner, in her book *Fragments of Isabella* (Ref. 27), tells vividly of her and her siblings' miraculous survival of these marches.

Resettlement and Rehabilitation

The US Army assumed responsibility for resettling about seven million refugees, so that by year's end their numbers were reduced to less than a million. A sizeable subset of that number constituted refugees who could not or would not return to their prewar homes. They became known as displaced persons (DPs).

Their rehabilitation, under the auspices of the US Army's Supreme Headquarters Allied Expeditionary Force (SHAEF), and subsequently under the United Nations Relief and Rehabilitation Agency (UNRRA), would last well into the early 1950s.

The number of DPs and their profiles would fluctuate during the next two years. For example, sizable numbers of Jewish DPs emigrated clandestinely to Palestine, or to a limited number of other countries that would accept them, mostly in the Americas, and with luck, to the United States or Canada. Immediately, new refugees would replenish the camps, often exceeding the number of those having departed. They represented people fleeing the grip of the Red Army, the new conqueror of eastern central Europe.

Commentary III

The Jewish Survivors

Introduction

At war's end, in May 1945, approximately four hundred thousand inmates had survived the horrors of the concentration and death camps and death marches (Ref. 42). Of that population, Jewish inmates constituted approximately ninety thousand. Assuming that the number of Jews who entered the concentration camps was, in total, at least as large as that of the non-Jews, the Jewish inmates who survived numbered less than a quarter of the non-Jewish. This reflects the deplorable condition of Jews *during* their incarceration. In the months following liberation, through the autumn of 1945, the number of Jewish survivors fell to approximately seventy thousand due to horrific living conditions and lack of medical supervision and care (Ref. 13).

The US Army failed to comprehend the unique state of Jewish survivors. The anti-Semitism prevalent in the US Army, from the rank of soldier up to the highest echelons, aggravated the despondency of Jewish survivors. General Patton, head of the US Third Army, responsible for maintaining the camps, gave weight to his anti-Semitic pronouncements by treating Jews more harshly than the other nationalities, despite Eisenhower's repeated reprimands. I later found that in October 1945, Eisenhower did relieve from duty his old West Point crony, George S. Patton. (Bill O'Reilly, in his book *Killing Patton: The Strange Death of World War II's Most Audacious General*, pays homage to Patton's audacity as well as to his propensity to defy authority. He reveals Patton as harbouring strong animosity against the Soviets and the intent to fight the Soviet Union, which may have led to his assassination by Stalin's agents in December 1945 (Ref. 32).)

Samples of Patton's Pronouncements

Others believe that the Displaced Person is a human being, which he is not, and this applies particularly to the Jews who are lower than animals (from

Patton's diary, following the release of the Harrison Report, circa August 1945).

> *...the Jewish type of DP is, in the majority of cases, a subhuman species without any of the cultural or social refinements of our time...*(from Patton's handwritten journal, in a letter responding to Eisenhower's, 1 October 1945 (Ref. 2).)

He erected new barbed-wire fences around the camps and ordered all Jews to be held inside, with no permits to leave, effectively enforcing the same appalling regimen they had endured before liberation.

Hilliard and Herman's Letters

> *...these human beings who literally have been in hell, who have no more than a vestige of life left, these Jews of Europe still need help, and they need it immediately...*(from Bob Hilliard and Ed Herman's letter (Ref. 17).)

Bob Hilliard (née Levine) and Ed Herman, two young, decorated Jewish soldiers – Bob, an Army newspaper editor, and Ed, a member of US Army intelligence and a 'wheeler-dealer' (as Hilliard describes him) – came to the fore to lay bare the ghastly state of Jewish survivors. These two Jewish GIs, of the Army's Ninth Air Corps battalion, were stationed at an air base not far from the just-established hospital at the church complex of St. Ottilien, near Landsberg, West Germany. (Landsberg, a few months following the Hilliard episode, became the foremost camp for Jewish DPs. That is where I, my sister, my brother-in-law, and his relatives landed toward the end of 1945 and where we stayed for more than a year.)

On 27 May 1945, Bob Hilliard attended the survivors' 'Liberation Concert' at the nearby hospital. That evening opened his eyes to the desperate condition of the 'surviving remnant' (*She'erit Hapletah*). The main address, delivered by Zalman Grinberg – a death-camp survivor and the head doctor, who would later become the chairman of the Central Committee of Liberated Jews – left a deep impression on Hilliard.

Hilliard collared his friend Ed Herman on the need for urgent action, leading to their letter-writing campaign. They mimeographed and sent out nearly one thousand copies of their letter to friends, relatives, political leaders, and Jewish philanthropists, skillfully avoiding – though barely – being court-martialled. Here are selected excerpts from the letter:

> Friends:
>   The Jews of Europe are a dying race. Even now, even after the defeat of Hitler and Nazism, they are slowly being exterminated from the face of the earth. YOU ARE TO BLAME! [for]…thousands of Jews in Europe who are today destitute, without food, shelter, clothing or medical aid.
>   …Today there are 750 people in the hospital, all of whom are receiving one-half the food they need to recover properly, sixty per cent of whom are confined to bed because they have no clothing to wear, others who are still wearing their concentration camp uniforms, all of whom are living with lice and disease because of the lack of bed clothing and equipment, and many of whom are not being cared for properly because of the lack of medicine.
>   …These surviving Jews of Europe want to live. We say they will live. WHAT DO YOU SAY?

One of their letters reportedly landed on President Truman's desk. In response to that letter – and others – Truman summoned Earl G. Harrison to represent him on a mission to investigate the condition of the camps.

Harrison soon arrived in Germany and toured the DP camps, accompanied by a number of on-site experts. His subsequent report, released in late August, outlined immediate steps to improve the situation in the DP camps, such as to remove barbed-wire fences and armed guards, to issue passes more liberally, and to hand over supervision and rehabilitation to UNRRA (United Nations Relief and Rehabilitation Administration). The report also recommended turning Landsberg and a number of other camps into camps for Jewish DPs, to avoid continued friction with their former enemies.

His report accused the US Army of neglecting the situation, describing in great detail the unique suffering of Jewish survivors at the hands of the Nazis and the critical need for the US Army to recognize that uniqueness. To quote Harrison: 'Jews as Jews (not as members of their nationality groups) have been more severely victimized than the non-Jewish members of the same or other nationalities…Refusal to recognize the Jews as such has the effect, in this situation, of closing one's eyes to their former and more barbaric persecution, which has already made them a separate group with greater needs.'

Harrison ended his report with a paragraph that would find its way into Truman's letter to Eisenhower, in which he stated that the Jews seemed to be in no better position than under the Nazis – except for the absence of gas chambers in the camps. (See *America and the Survivors of the Holocaust* by Leonard Dinnerstein, for the full text of the report (Ref. 5).)

The Harrison Report made the headlines of the *New York Times* and other leading US newspapers. It prompted President Truman to send a scathing letter to General Eisenhower on 31 August. The letter pointed out that SHAEF's humane policies with regard to the DP camps were not being carried out, and provided egregious examples of it. The president pointed out in particular the need to remedy the situation of the Jewish DPs. He ordered Eisenhower to institute inspection tours to make sure that his subordinates carried out the remedial steps and concluded by asking the general to report to him on the implementation of his orders.

The letter had a clarion-call effect on Eisenhower and his Expeditionary Force, and it became a turning point for rehabilitation of Jewish inmates in the camps. In effect, the army began to single out the Jews as a distinct nationality and to provide new camps or modify existing ones exclusively for them.

The DP Camps and Population

In October 1945, the US Army transferred control of the DP camps to UNRRA. Following is a brief summary of the number of camps in Germany at the time of transfer of control.

Upon transfer, the US Occupation Zone in West Germany had thirty DP camps with an average of approximately two thousand DPs each. The British and French zones had three camps each. The number of camps and inmates kept growing in the following two years, with tens of thousands of Jews leaving the Soviet Union, as well as others fleeing Eastern European countries in fear of the advancing Red Army. The new waves of Jewish refugees swelled, eventually exceeding the capacity of the existing camps. Additional camps sprung up in Austria and Italy to accommodate the new arrivals. The total number of Jewish DPs continued to increase, to several hundred thousand, until 1948, when many migrated to the newly-formed state of Israel, or to the Americas.

Commentary IV

UNRRA and the NGOs

The official formation of UNRRA (United Nations Relief and Rehabilitation Administration) had taken place at a White House gathering of representatives of the forty-four UN member nations in November 1943. Its mission was to care for the homeless casualties of the war. UNRRA served as our redeemer. It assumed control from the US Army of the Landsberg and other DP camps. It furnished our food and shelter; it funded our cultural and professional training. It provided the platform for the NGOs, the nongovernmental organizations which focused on specific services, defined by their resources and areas of competence.

To wit:

The Joint – the American Jewish Joint Distribution Committee – founded in 1914 to provide assistance to Jews living in Palestine under Turkish rule, became my immediate companion during my travels home, as well as later during my stay in the DP camp.

The Hebrew Immigrant Aid Society (HIAS), an American charitable organization originally founded in response to the exodus of Jewish refugees from Imperial Russia in the late nineteenth and early twentieth centuries, assisted me upon my arrival in the United States.

Bricha (escape or flight in Hebrew), formed in 1944, helped Jewish Holocaust survivors illegally escape post-Second World War Europe to Palestine, evading the British ban on Jewish immigration. Bricha trained Moniek's cousin, Naftali Eckstein, among many other volunteers. They helped remnants of the Perlman family in Krakow, as well as Luba and me, illegally cross the borders of Czechoslovakia, Austria and Germany, to reach Landsberg am Lech in 1945 and 1946.

Agudath Israel, founded in 1912, was an Orthodox Jewish organization that acted to secure religious rights for Jews worldwide. They assisted religious people, like my brother-in-law Moniek Perlman, to get kosher food and other religious articles, particularly for holidays.

The Organization for Rehabilitation and Training (ORT), started in 1880, provides technical training and education for young Jewish people.

It played a key role in transforming uprooted Jewish youths in the DP camps, including myself, into skilled technicians.

B'nai B'rith, an American fraternal organization, has provided social and financial assistance to needy Jewish communities worldwide since its founding in 1843. In 1924 it adopted Hillel, a campus organization for Jewish students. Indeed, B'nai B'rith-Hillel secured my scholarship to come to Colby College in 1947. (Hillel is presently an independent unit.)

B'nai B'rith-Hillel Scholarships

In 1946 the B'nai B'rith-Hillel Foundation, under the leadership of Dr. Abram Sachar (later founder and president of Brandeis University), appointed Marie Syrkin, a prominent American educator and Zionist, to comb the DP camps for worthy young Jewish DPs. The results of her search culminated in the admission of several dozen young people to US colleges on scholarships. I was one of the lucky recipients.

Hashomer Hatzair

Hashomer Hatzair (the Young Guard), a Socialist-Zionist youth movement founded in 1913 in Austria, furnished training for Jewish survivors in so-called kibbutzim (communal farming settlements). The training centres prepared the members for agricultural and other vocations in Palestine. The kibbutz provided my food and lodging for most of my stay in Landsberg. There, I also honed my farming skills, which I had first learned as a very young man.

Commentary V

Major Heymont, the Rehabilitator of the Landsberg DP Camp

Landsberg am Lech, some forty miles from Munich, adjoined the Dachau concentration/death camp complex and served as military housing of the Wehrmacht during the war. It soon became the second largest camp for DPs in the American zone of West Germany, with approximately five thousand Jews in dire need of rehabilitation.

Major Irving Heymont, a twenty-seven-year-old army officer, arrived at Landsberg on 19 September 1945, with orders from General Eisenhower to 'clean up the camp'. The camp had drawn particular ire from the army's high command, having been the source of many of the criticisms of the army in Earl Harrison's report on the mistreatment of Jewish DPs. In the following eighty days, Major Heymont assiduously wrote almost daily letters to his wife, describing his ordeal and the dismal state of the camp and its inhabitants (Ref. 15). Here are his observations on the evening of his arrival:

> The camp is filthy beyond description. Sanitation is virtually unknown. Words fail me when I try to think of an adequate description. The camp is run by an UNRRA Team and a few representatives of the American Joint…These people have been working against very great obstacles. The army units we relieved obviously did nothing more than insure that rations were delivered to the camp. With a few exceptions, the people of the camp themselves appear demoralized beyond hope of rehabilitation. They appear to be beaten both spiritually and physically, with no hopes or incentives for the future…There are a few courageous ones left among them who have organized a camp committee to try to do something.

He went on to describe his meeting with the camp committee, during which he presented his policies and expectations. He explained, 'the army came to Europe to fight the Nazis and not to stand guard over their victims' and stated that he expected Landsberg to become a self-governing community 'with the army present only to help'. For the immediate tasks, he ordered the committee to prepare plans 'for improved sanitation, firefighting, betterment of the schools, establishment of central messes…and increasing the number of people available for work'. He concludes the letter noting, 'what they seem to need is friendship and understanding'.

To that end, he began to look actively for Yiddish-speaking Jewish soldiers to help him bridge the inmates' mistrust of any authority.

In his second letter, he noted being shocked at the iron fence, augmented with barbed wire and patrolled by armed soldiers from the outside perimeter, and the sight of confined DPs peering through the fence at Germans walking about freely. The barracks, well-designed for housing military units, 'could not be worse for housing families'. The absence of partitions in the huge rooms, and particularly in the communal latrines, robbed people of privacy. The toilets beggared description. The water pressure was low because of war damage to the water mains. In the washrooms, most of the sinks, clogged with food scraps, were rendered out of order.

A man of action as well as great compassion, Heymont dramatically transformed the camp and its inmates to near normalcy in the ensuing approximately eight weeks. He orchestrated, as a top priority, the clean-up and set-up of sanitation programmes; eliminated the prison-like constraints on the DPs' movements; improved cooking and dining facilities; reshaped family-unit quarters; organized free and fair elections for self government; promoted training and educational programmes at all levels; and opened multiple venues to meet the social, cultural, spiritual and recreational needs of the DPs.

His most telling accomplishment was that he succeeded, with permission of the high command, to establish Landsberg as a strictly Jewish camp. This ended the quarrelsome state that had existed between Jewish and non-Jewish DPs, who continued to harbour deep, innate hostilities against the Jews.

In short, by the time Major Heymont left on 6 December 1945, Landsberg DP camp in West Germany had become the model for a well-functioning, self-governing community full of energy and hopefulness.

Epilogue

In September 1948, I entered MIT's main, domed building. As I walked its hallowed halls in those early days, I passed with awe famous men of science and engineering: mathematicians Drs. John von Neumann and Vasily Wiener; physicists Drs. Francis Weston Sears and Victor Weisskopf; electrical engineers Drs. Vannevar Bush and Julius Adams Stratton, along with a number of others.

My own professors, whom I would soon get to know, bore impressive names and credits as well: Dr. Warren K. Lewis, dubbed the father of chemical engineering and Professor Edward R. Gilliland, co-inventor of the technology that processes crude oil for gasoline production, which had become essential for winning the war against Hitler.

I completed my chemical engineering degree in 1951. I then began my graduate studies while working in the Fuels Research Laboratory of Professor Hoyt C. Hottel.

In the summer of 1951, I attended an international student fair at Harvard where a bright, vivacious and attractive woman caught my attention. With her red hair, smattering of freckles and wide brown eyes, Regina, though petite, possessed a commanding, confident presence. Her experiences, as it turned out, mirrored mine. She and her family had fled their home near Warsaw and, a couple of years later, landed in Osh, Kyrgyzstan. There, she was able to enroll in the Moscow University Medical School, which had been evacuated to Kyrgyzstan, and at war's end returned to Moscow. A couple years later, she rejoined her family to return to Poland. Like me, she found her hometown devastated and devoid of Jews. She emigrated to the United States in 1947, sponsored by relatives.

After two years of study, she graduated from Simmons College and soon went to work as a medical technician for Harvard professor Sydney Farber, who was doing research on pediatric leukemia and who would later become known as the father of modern chemotherapy. Impressed by Regina's work, the young professor recommended that she enter Harvard Medical School, which she completed in 1952.

In the winter of 1952, Regina and I married. During the next few years, she gave birth to our two older children, Mark and May. She also completed her residency, and we moved to Paramus, New Jersey, where she began to practise pediatrics while I worked as a chemical engineer. In 1959, Regina gave birth to our third child, David, and two years later, to our youngest boy, Ted.

I began my career as a chemical engineer with M.W. Kellogg, a consulting company for the petroleum industry. During my initial assignment, I co-developed the first computer application tool for equipment design called 'The Flexible Flow Sheet', which short-circuited the design of complex equipment to a few minutes, from the weeks that it had taken engineers to do by hand. A few years later, Esso Engineering recruited me to head their RECAP (Research and Engineering Computer Applications) double-digit group, to modernize their process-engineering software.

As the years went by, however, I found the bureaucratic environment stifling. At the same time, my drive to create independently got the best of me. I left Esso and opened a computer school. For a time, I felt that I was riding a wave of success. Alas, it was short-lived.

In the fall of 1968, Regina required surgery to remove a suspicious lump in her breast. It turned out to be malignant and her radiologist predicted at most six months' survival. I was devastated by the news, of course, which was then compounded by having to sell my computer school. The fear of impending financial ruin plunged me into depression. A few months later, however, like the proverbial phoenix, I rose and regained my footing, thanks to an old friend who found me a high-level position at Mobil Oil, which I began in 1971.

Regina fought her disease much longer than predicted, but succumbed in 1973. The children were crushed, as was I. She had loomed over all our lives, and her death left an immense void in the family.

After her death, I relocated with the children to East Brunswick, New Jersey, to be closer to my work with Mobil in Princeton. The following decade presented enormous challenges for me as a single parent, and, in time, I was compelled to seek, with the children, professional counselling.

Meanwhile, I went on to the role of senior technical adviser in the engineering department at Mobil and was put in charge of revising the 'bible' of data and methods used for refinery design and operations-control worldwide. As part of this, I co-developed the 'Lee-Kesler Correlations', published in the *AIChE* (American Institute of Chemical Engineering)

Journal in 1976. In 2006, the journal's special centennial issue listed those correlations as Number 6 of the 100 most-referenced publications in the journal.

In 1979 I founded Kesler Engineering, Inc. (KEI) to develop software for the petroleum industry. The tools I developed earlier in my career helped me and my associates design similar tools for use on the personal computers which were gradually replacing the old mainframes.

My urge to go independent stemmed from my invention of a way to lump components in distillation involving hundreds, or even thousands, of individual components, characterizing the mixture to be distilled. The need to rigorously handle all these components would require expensive computers (called super computers). The invention would use, at most, a dozen lumps to characterize the mixture and reduce that time a thousand-fold or even a million-fold.

In the summer of 1984, I met an attractive, dynamic and brilliant brunette, Barbara Reed. She had come to the area a year earlier to join the Department of Journalism and Media Studies at Rutgers University. I became enamoured with her quick, insightful mind, her energy and her values. A niece of famous Jewish philosopher and theologian Dr. Abraham Joshua Heschel, Barbara opened my eyes to a broader, deeper and more nuanced view of Judaism and its relation to other faiths. She soon became my intellectual and spiritual soul mate, and in October 1985 we married, and I became the stepfather of sixteen-year-old Michael and eleven-year-old Esther. The next few years provided us with opportunities to blend our two families, although my own children, being older, were often away working or studying.

The two decades following our wedding brought us deep personal fulfilment and a comfortable lifestyle. We married off and helped settle all six of our children and saw the addition of our first grandchild, a boy born to my oldest son and his wife. Our family network of in-laws and close relatives extended across the country and beyond. We travelled for business, but more often for pleasure, from coast to coast and across all the continents (except Antarctica). In short, we prospered.

The march of time, however, began to perniciously invade my life. During the last few years of my career, I suffered progressive vision loss due to glaucoma. Week to week, I struggled more and more to recognize on the computer screen intricate diagrams and figures essential to my work, forcing me to walk away from my chemical engineering business. In 2004, I sold my company to General Physics, an NYSE corporation, and pursued consulting work with the firm. Two years later, I retired.

With a strong need to remain productive, I migrated to a new vocation: the writing of my experiences during the Second World War. Being blind, I hired secretarial and research help. Gradually, I mastered the routine of dictating the text and reviewing it later, as my assistant read it back to me.

During the next several years, I edited my late wife's unfinished wartime memoir, *Grit* (Ref. 21); wrote of my own war experiences in *Shards of War* (Ref. 22); and of my family's difficulties after their mother Regina's death in *Hurdles*.

This book – based in small part on my earlier writings – addresses the last twelve months of the war and its immediate aftermath: the displaced persons camp, and beyond. It depicts that part of my harrowing saga against the backdrop of the raging conflagration of the Second World War.

Writing is a lonely vocation, and quite tiring. The quiet hours of thinking and re-thinking passages in my book gave me the opportunity to rediscover another arrow in my quiver: my vocal training and experience as the cantor in a large, growing Jewish community in Paramus, forty years earlier.

I resumed my musical activities, assembling a small group of professional musicians with whom I present annual concerts at the East Brunswick Public Library and other venues. These events celebrate the rich cultural legacy of the Jews of Eastern and Central Europe, country by country. They draw a full house and are a source of great pleasure for me. They also buttress my mission to bear witness to the atrocities suffered by my people, as well as to fight for a better, just world. On 24 October 2018, the East Brunswick Public Library Foundation honoured me at a special gala event to recognize my five years of contributing to the community with these enriching presentations.

In 2015 Barbara retired from her thirty-plus years as a professor of Journalism and Media Studies at Rutgers University. A lighter, more relaxed climate has imbued our household. We have more time to visit and be with our six children and eleven grandchildren, spread all over the United States.

I have lived in East Brunswick for more than four decades, and Barbara more than three. We're active members of several congregations in the area, and enjoy a circle of close friends and acquaintances with whom we share a wide array of interests and activities. We are grateful that the state of our minds and bodies still permits us to bring meaningful content to each day.

The Travails and Rewards of Luba and Moniek

In 1947, Luba, her husband, Moniek and their infant, Nathan, left Germany and joined my aunt and her family in Montevideo, Uruguay. Moniek continued as an inventor, developing a new design for electric shavers, which he worked to manufacture and market, while Luba taught in the local Hebrew school. A year later, they moved to Buenos Aires, Argentina, where they lived for the next two years. In November 1950 the family, including four-year-old Nathan and a baby daughter, came to the United States, sponsored by my good friends, the Saltzes.

They settled into a small apartment in Manhattan and later relocated to Brooklyn, where Moniek found work as a toolmaker for Ideal, a toy manufacturing company. After incurring an injury to his back, Moniek was laid up for nearly a year. During that time, Luba, with Moniek's help, assembled Swiss watches, and this activity became, essentially, their source of income.

While bedridden, Moniek learned of the booming industry for assembling zippers, reckoning that most of the time-consuming, manual operations could be automated. With his health restored, he invented and built machines to automate zipper assembly. For the next twenty-five years he and Luba, as his business partner, proceeded to manufacture thousands of these machines and market them worldwide. In 1980, with sixty patents to Moniek's name and 120 workers in their factory, Moniek and Luba sold their business to a subsidiary of ICI, a major British chemical manufacturer.

Luba passed away in 2012 at the age of ninety, leaving behind a sizable progeny. Moniek suffered several years from the ravages of old age before passing away in 2016, at ninety-six, surrounded by a close-knit, loving family. His and Luba's descendants, now nearly fifty in number, include three dozen great-grandchildren, now approaching marriageable age – in the setting of Orthodox communities where people marry young and raise large families.

In 2005, Luba had prepared a tape of reminiscences of our war experiences. This tape, along with the numerous discussions I'd had with Luba and Moniek over the years, laid the groundwork for this book. Indeed, Luba's uncanny memory helped me to uncover a wealth of memories buried by layers of cobwebs, spun by time.

My Friend Joseph Gitman's Legacy

Joseph Gitman, my senior by some seven years, had become my spiritual mentor and, in many ways, acted as an older brother to me during the two years following the war. Together we had walked the empty streets of Dubno, lamenting the loss of its Jewish community. We embraced each other in tears and said Kaddish at the mass grave of our parents. We spent more hopeful times in the Landsberg DP camp and, later, in Paris. And we continued our friendship in the United States.

Joseph was brought to this country by his cousins and found a position as a rabbi in a community near Hartford, Connecticut. He also enrolled at Yale University, where he obtained his PhD in history. His thesis on the Polish press and the Jewish problem in Poland before the war won him prestigious awards. A decade after his arrival in the United States, he became a professor at the Merchant Marine Academy in Kings Point, New York. My first wife and I attended his wedding to Carolyn, a talented photographer and a Connecticut native. Barbara and I visited him and his family, which went on to include a daughter and a son, on numerous occasions in Great Neck, and we welcomed them in our home often as well.

In 1990, Joseph and Carolyn married off their son, Eliyahu, who emigrated with his bride to Israel. A year or so later, Joseph retired, and he and Carolyn joined the newly-weds, moving into a retirement community near Jerusalem. My communication with Joseph came to a halt in 2004 when he passed away at the age of ninety-five. His son and daughter-in-law, Sarah, are doing well and have borne ten children to 'avenge' the deaths of their grandparents and relatives in Dubno.

Osher Balaban

Osher Balaban came to the Landsberg Displaced Persons Camp about six months after my sister and me with his wife, Zhenya, a nurse whom he had met while injured in Stalingrad. Osher, Luba's schoolmate from Dubno who prepared false documents for me in Samarkand, helped Luba engineer my escape from the Soviet army.

We became close friends in Landsberg, and nearly three decades later, Osher and Zhenya entertained us in their home in Ramat Gan, Israel, with two of their boys present. Sadly, their oldest boy, summoned from his medical studies in Belgium for immediate return to the army, was killed in the Sinai during the 1973 Arab-Israeli War, the day after his return.

We visited the couple again several times whenever we visited Israel. Osher went to work as a high school mathematics teacher, working long hours in two schools. Zhenya was gainfully employed as a nurse. They took great pride in their lovely home, their married boys and in Israel itself. I still remember well Osher's authoritative pronouncement: 'Israel will have peace when the Arabs are ready for it.' Zhenya died in the mid 1990s. Osher, I believe, died in 2005. Barbara and I miss them both dearly.

Postface

Thanksgiving 2016 brought tears of joy to me. Together with our six children, their spouses and eleven grandchildren, Barbara and I celebrated the holiday in Westwood, near Boston, in the spacious home of our oldest son, Mark, and his wife, Peggy. My joy derived from thankfulness that Mark was functioning again as the host, proud of his culinary abilities. A year earlier, two strokes in succession had nearly cost Mark his life. I remembered how I saw him then, unable to speak, walk or fully use his hands. For the next several months, I mobilized my own resources, to the extent that I could, to help him recover. Alas, his rehabilitation proved slow and painful. That period – the fear of losing him – was as painful as any I had experienced in my long life. That Thanksgiving, filled with lively banter and good humor, celebrated not only Mark's recovery but also his birthday.

When it came my turn to express thanks, I stood and recollected to the twenty-plus family members and friends at the table how I had arrived in the United States in 1947 with fifty dollars in my pocket, no friends, no knowledge of the language, all alone. I expressed my gratitude for being surrounded by a close and loving family. I also conveyed my satisfaction about almost having completed my new manuscript.

After I sat back down, my mind wandered to my parents. I felt a pang in my gut for how hungry they must have been while living in the ghetto. I remembered witnessing the mass grave on the outskirts of Dubno that contained their remains. I could almost hear them crying out to me, imploring me to share my recollections of the ugly calamity that extinguished two-thirds of European Jewry.

My painful thoughts receded as I began to reflect on the kindness that fate had bestowed upon me. Burning wings had lifted this sapling from the ashes and carried it all the way to this blessed country, where I set down roots and gave rise to the magnificent family before me.

I asked myself, *What drove you to expend resources and thousands of hours writing a book at an age when most people would be preparing peacefully for the end of life?* The desire to pass along to my progeny, friends and others the details of my harrowing past. *And where does that desire come from?* My origins as a Jew.

I had an epiphany: The Jews had been *born to inform.*

Jewish legend has it that our forefather, Abraham, was the first to introduce to the world the concept of one God. Further, he had the audacity to plead with God, to argue with God on a personal basis. Throughout millennia, this evolved to the core of Jewish thinking and culture, propagating endless, voluminous commentaries to the basic idea.

I chuckled, remembering the hours I had spent in my youth with a rebbe (teacher) pouring over pages of the first major commentaries of the Bible (the Talmud), filled with arguments and counter-arguments, often concerning minutiae. It showed, however, an obsessive devotion to open discussion, free expression and uninhibited thinking and inquiry, which challenged conventional norms and wisdom. It also became the fountain for Jewish creativity and ingenuity. Abraham's penchant for audacious inquiry and open expression provided a foundation for the prophet Isaiah to plead passionately for goodwill and justice between men and peace between nations. It empowered the noted twentieth-century Jewish theologian Abraham Joshua Heschel to construct a modern philosophy of religion rooted in the ancient and medieval Jewish traditions.

Likewise, the compelling impulse to inform pervades Prophet Jeremiah's lamentations on the destruction of the Temple, as it does in the heartrending account of the Auschwitz inferno by Elie Wiesel. Walter Isaacson, in his definitive biography *Einstein: His Life and Universe*, highlights the pivotal role Judaism played in freeing Albert Einstein to divine the cosmo-dynamic laws that govern the stars'/planets' orbits and their interactions. Einstein codified these laws in his theory of relativity. They predicted, for example, that light had the power to deflect a planet's trajectory. The 1919 total eclipse stunningly confirmed that prediction and the event heaped acclaim on Einstein as the greatest scientist of all time.

No wonder that the Jews, with a miniscule less than one-tenth per cent of the world's population, have gained over twenty per cent of the Nobel prizes. Indeed, I feel proud, yet humble, to carry on my forebears' legacy.

Bibliography/References

1. Bendersky, Joseph W., *The Jewish Threat: Anti-Semitic Politics of the U.S. Army* (New York: Basic Books, Perseus Books Group, 2000).
2. Blumenson, Martin, *The Patton Papers: 1940–1945* (Boston: Houghton Mifflin Company, 1974).
3. Dawidowicz, Lucy S., *The War Against the Jews: 1933–1945* (New York: Holt, Rinehart and Winston, 1975).
4. Desbois, Patrick, *The Holocaust by Bullets: A Priest's Journey to Uncover the Truth Behind the Murder of 1.5 Million Jews* (New York: Palgrave Macmillan, 2008).
5. Dinnerstein, Leonard, *America and the Survivors of the Holocaust* (New York: Columbia University Press, 1982).
6. Dobbs, Michael, *Six Months in 1945: FDR, Stalin, Churchill, and Truman – From World War to Cold War* (New York: Alfred A. Knopf, 2012).
7. Ehrenburg, Ilya and Grossman, Vasily, *The Complete Black Book of Russian Jewry* (New Brunswick: Transaction Publishers, 2003).
8. Erickson, John, *The Road to Stalingrad, Stalin's War with Germany: Volume 1* (New Haven: Yale University Press, 1975).
9. Genirberg, Sam, *Among the Enemy: Hiding in Plain Sight in Nazi Germany* (Los Gatos, CA: Robertson Publishing, 2012).
10. Gilbert, Martin, *The Holocaust: A History of the Jews of Europe During the Second World War* (New York: Holt, Rinehart and Winston, 1985).
11. Glantz, David M., *The Initial Period of War on the Eastern Front, 22 June–August 1941: Proceedings of the Fourth Art of War Symposium* (London: Frank Cass & Co, 1993).
12. Gottfried, Ted, *Displaced Persons: The Liberation and Abuse of Holocaust Survivors* (Brookfield, CT: Twenty-First Century Books, 2001).
13. Grossmann, Atina, *Jews, Germans, and Allies: Close Encounters in Occupied Germany* (Princeton: Princeton University Press, 2007).
14. Hastings, Max, *Armageddon: The Battle for Germany, 1944–1945* (New York: A.A. Knopf, 2004).
15. Heymont, Irving, *Among the Survivors of the Holocaust, 1945: The Landsberg DP Camp Letters of Major Irving Heymont, United States Army* (Cincinnati, OH: The American Jewish Archives, 1982).
16. Hilberg, Raul, *The Destruction of the European Jews,* Third Edition (New Haven: Yale University Press, 2003).
17. Hilliard, Robert L., *Surviving the Americans: The Continued Struggle of the Jews After Liberation* (New York: Seven Stories Press, 1997).
18. Judt, Tony, *Postwar: A History of Europe Since 1945* (New York: The Penguin Press, 2005).
19. Kavanaugh, Sarah, *ORT, The Second World War and the Rehabilitation of Holocaust Survivors* (London/Portland, OR: Vallentine Mitchell, 2008).

20. Keneally, Thomas, *Schindler's List* (New York: Simon & Schuster, 1982).

21. Kesler, Michael G. (Ed.), *Grit: A Pediatrician's Odyssey From a Soviet Camp to Harvard* (Bloomington, IN: Author House, 2009).

22. Kesler, Michael G., *Shards of War – Fleeing To & From Uzbekistan* (Durham, CT: Strategic Book Group, 2010).

23. Kessner, Carole S., *Marie Syrkin: Values Beyond the Self* (Waltham, MA: Brandeis University Press, 2008).

24. Knight, Amy, *Beria: Stalin's First Lieutenant* (Princeton: Princeton University Press, 1993).

25. Koestler, Arthur, *Darkness at Noon* (New York: Bantam Books, 1968).

26. Kulischer, Eugene M., *Europe on the Move: War and Population Changes, 1917–47* (New York: Columbia University Press, 1948).

27. Leitner, Isabella, *Fragments of Isabella: A Memoir of Auschwitz* (New York: Open Road Media, 2018).

28. Mankowitz, Zeev W., *Life Between Memory and Hope: The Survivors of the Holocaust in Occupied Germany* (Cambridge: Cambridge University Press, 2002).

29. Marrus, Michael R., *The Unwanted: European Refugees in the Twentieth Century* (New York, Oxford: Oxford University Press, 1985).

30. Meltyukhov, Mikhail, *Stalin's Missed Chance* (Saarbrücken, Germany: VDM Publishing, 2010).

31. Morris, Rob, *Untold Valor: Forgotten Stories of American Bomber Crews Over Europe in World War II* (Washington, D.C.: Potomac Books, Inc., 2006).

32. O'Reilly, Bill and Dugard, Martin, *Killing Patton: The Strange Death of World War II's Most Audacious General* (New York: Henry Holt and Company, 2014).

33. Patt, Avinoam J. and Berkowitz, Michael (Eds), *'We Are Here': New Approaches to Jewish Displaced Persons in Germany* (Detroit: Wayne State University Press, 2010).

34. Person, Katarzyna, *ORT and the Rehabilitation of Holocaust Survivors: ORT Activities 1945–1956* (London: World ORT, 2012).

35. Proudfoot, Malcolm J., *European Refugees, 1939–52: A Study in Forced Population Movement* (Evanston, IL: Northwestern University Press, 1956).

36. Rubenstein, Joshua and Altman, Ilya (Eds), *The Unknown Black Book: The Holocaust in the German-Occupied Soviet Territories* (Bloomington, IN: Indiana University Press, 2010).

37. Sachar, Abram L., *The Redemption of the Unwanted* (New York: St. Martin's/Marek, 1983).

38. Schwarz, Leo W., *The Redeemers: A Saga of the Years 1945–1952* (New York: Farrar, Straus and Young, 1953).

39. Service, Robert, *Stalin: A Biography* (Cambridge: The Belknap Press of Harvard University Press, 2005).

40. Shephard, Ben, *The Long Road Home: The Aftermath of the Second World War* (New York: Alfred A. Knopf, 2011).

41. Shirer, William L., *The Rise and Fall of the Third Reich: A History of Nazi Germany* (New York: Touchstone, 1981).

42. Stone, Dan, *The Liberation of the Camps: The End of the Holocaust and Its Aftermath* (New Haven and London: Yale University Press, 2015).

43. Wyman, Mark, *DPs: Europe's Displaced Persons, 1945–1951* (London and Toronto: Associated University Presses, 1989).

44. Yahil, Leni, *The Holocaust: The Fate of European Jewry* (New York, Oxford: Oxford University Press, 1990).

45. Zhukov, Georgy and Roberts, Geoffrey (Eds), *Marshal of Victory: The Autobiography of General Georgy Zhukov* (United Kingdom: Pen & Sword Books, Ltd., 2013).

46. Zimering, Sabina S., *Hiding in the Open: A Holocaust Memoir* (St. Cloud, MN: North Star Press of St. Cloud, Inc., 2001).

Online Sources
Articles

47. *Killing Centers.* n.d. in Holocaust Encyclopedia, United States Holocaust Museum, https://www.ushmm.org/wlc/en/article.php?ModuleId=10007327

48. *Ohrdruf.* n.d. in Holocaust Encyclopedia, United States Holocaust Museum, https://www.ushmm.org/wlc/en/article.php?ModuleId=10006131

49. Smilovitsky, Dr. Leonid, *Ilya Ehrenburg on the Holocaust in Belarus: Unknown Testimony.* 1999, Jewish Gen Belarus SIG Online Newsletter, October 2002 http://www.jewishgen.org/Belarus/newsletters/misc/IlyaEhrenburg/index.html

50. *The Atlantic Conference & Charter, 1941.* n.d.in Milestones: 1937-1945, U.S.A. Department of State, Office of the Historian, https://history.state.gov/milestones/1937-1945/atlantic-conf

51. *The Irgun: Bombing of the King David Hotel (July 22 1946).* n.d. in Jewish Virtual Library, http://www.jewishvirtuallibrary.org/bombing-of-the-king-david-hotel

52. *Exodus 1947.* n.d. in Holocaust Encyclopedia, United States Holocaust Museum, https://www.ushmm.org/wlc/en/article.php?ModuleId=10005419

53. Axelrod, Alan, *Casualties in World War II.* Encyclopedia of World War II, Vol. 1. NewYork: Facts On File, 2013. *Modern World History Online.* Web. 17 June 2015, http://online.infobase.com/HRC/Search/Details/264638?q=civilian deaths World War II

54. *Landsberg* n.d. in ORT and the Displaced Persons Camps, World ORT 2010, https://dpcamps.ort.org/camps/germany/us-zone/

Film

55. *Yalta Conference 1945.* British Pathé Archive, Film ID 1997.06, https://www.britishpathe.com/video/yalta-conference

Maps

POLAND 1921-1939: http://info-poland.buffalo.edu/classroom/maps/map39.jpg
From Lviv, Ukraine to Samarkand, Uzbekistan:
    https://www.google.com/maps/@43.7028791,27.5840049,4z
Uzbekistan: http://www.nationsonline.org/oneworld/map/uzbekistan-political-map.htm

Appendix

Testimony of a Survivor of the Dubno Ghetto

Note: In 1995, the East Brunswick Jewish Center in New Jersey held a service to commemorate the Holocaust, under the title 'Dubno, a Shtetl No More'. Mrs. Irene Tannen, a lawyer and survivor of the Dubno ghetto, was invited to address the gathering. Following is a record of Irene's remarks.

***

We are assembled today for a memorial service for the parents and family members of Michael Kesler, Harold Greenspan, mine, and all the thousands and thousands of Jews who had been killed during the Nazi-occupation time in our hometown Dubno, Poland, and all other places.

Michael Kesler and Harold Greenspan gave you a background about our hometown and the events which followed immediately after the Germans crossed the Soviet border Sunday, June 22, 1941. Michael and Harold did not have to witness the human degradation, the life in the ghetto, the everyday atrocities, the selection processes, and finally the deaths of the beloved. I had witnessed all of these; I survived.

When Michael Kesler approached me to share the ghetto experiences, it was for me an emotional decision. During the more than fifty years which elapsed, I tried to suppress all these memories. After Michael's approach, I started to reconstruct the events. Here they are:

Sunday, June 22, 1941, and Monday, young men were being drafted. The Soviet administration – police, city hall, and others – were nervous waiting for directions from higher authorities. The high officials were putting their families on trains and trucks heading east. Jewish families were gathering to decide what to do – to stay or to escape; where to escape; how to escape; who of the family should escape. Big decisions, emotional decisions. The main concern of each family was the young people whom they considered to be most vulnerable. On June 24, 1941, we heard already some artillery activity, and on June 25, the first SS *Einsatzgruppen* arrived in Dubno.

Two days later, the *Einsatzgruppen* swept the Jewish quarter and, with the assistance of the local Ukrainian paramilitary gangs, rounded up close to eight hundred Jewish males. They were marched to the Jewish cemetery, summarily executed, and their bodies thrown into huge dugouts. Among these men was my older brother, who left behind his young wife and a three-year-old girl, Miriam. Among those men was also the father of my girlfriend with whom I survived, Rafael Bogdanow. The terror and the panic among the Jews were unbearable.

During the first week of invasion, the SS people began to organize the persecution and ultimate execution of the Jewish community. They established a *Judenrat* – a Jewish representation body – and they forced the *Judenrat* to submit names of the best-known and honorable Jews in town. These people were picked up and hanged in the town center. Then, the German authorities issued an order for all Jews to wear an armband with the Star of David. This was followed by another order for Jews to deliver to the authorities all jewelry in their possession.

Then came the selection process of girls and young women. It began with the SS running through the Jewish homes and rounding up young women and girls into one crowded area. The SS people also searched in places around the house where young women might be hiding. They herded the crowd and women on the street – whoever was there at the time – into a large restaurant. Following that, the SS searched for and apprehended women who had escaped and were hiding in surrounding areas. These women were also brought to the restaurant.

I was there. The SS were like wild animals. We were beaten with whips and forced into adjoining rooms. After many hours we were released. However, many of the victims disappeared and were never heard from again.

While these atrocities were going on, the Jews had to work to get food. We sold whatever we could. Sometime in the middle of July, the German government forcibly transported the Jews from the surrounding small towns to Dubno and placed them in designated areas along the whole length of Stara Street and its neighboring narrow side streets. This was the beginning of the Dubno ghetto.

In the winter of 1941, we all were in the ghetto. There was not enough food, the quarters were cold, and the older people and the children were getting ill and dying. The designated area for the Jews, the ghetto, was small. During the winter of 1941, the Jews had to deliver furs to the German authorities. One of our school friends was arrested and shot because he was listening to news on the radio. It is hard for a human being to imagine the everyday life in the ghetto, the struggle to survive during the day and to see the beloved again in the evening. During that time, several 'actions' took place with several-thousand people herded, marched out of the ghetto, then shot and buried in the ravines at the outskirts of Dubno.

In the late summer of 1942, a large-scale 'action' by the SS squads inflicted horrible deaths of nearly three thousand in the Dubno ghetto. I escaped during this action. The final liquidation of the Dubno ghetto was in October 1942. Several dozens of our brothers and sisters managed to escape the slaughter. They found refuge in the villages of mainly Czech and some Polish peasants who, in many cases, paid with their own lives and the lives of their families to save Jews. In my family, two children of my older sister found refuge in the winter of 1943 in a Czech small village of about thirty families. The villagers decided that the children, ages seven and eight, would be every week in a different household. This lasted for over a year, and all the villagers, including the children, kept secret that the two Jewish children were hiding in their midst.

Index of Names

(in order of appearance)

Lightning Source UK Ltd.
Milton Keynes UK
UKHW021122160221
378865UK00006B/136